CONTEMPORARY SHORTHAND

by

Roy B. Tabor

© 2004 by Roy B. Tabor. All rights reserved.

No part of this book may be reproduced, stored in a retrieval system, or transmitted by any means, electronic, mechanical, photocopying, recording, or otherwise, without written permission from the author.

First published by AuthorHouse 05/03/04

ISBN: 1-4184-6271-3 (e-book)
ISBN: 1-4184-4059-0 (Paperback)

Library of Congress Control Number: 2003092166

This book is printed on acid free paper.

Printed in the United States of America
Bloomington, IN

CONTENTS

Introduction v

Part One: Fundamental principles

1: Writing the sound of words 2
2: The vowel system...4

Part Two Basic Mode

3: Writing consonants..7
4: Writing the word outline 10
5: Quick forms...14
6: Writing T and D 16
7: The sound of R 22
8: The sounds of S and Z..28
9: The sound of L 33
10: H and its combinations...38
11: The sound of 'shun'...42
12: Vowels and Diphthongs 45
13: The '-ng' ending..49
14: All about X 53
15: Double vowels...57
16: Abbreviating principles 64
17: Writing TR 68
18: Useful prefixes 74
19: Useful suffixes 77
20: All about numbers...81

Part Three Alpha script level

21: Writing Alpha level...87
22: Writing T and D 93
23: The sound of R 97
24: The sounds of S and Z..102
25: The L endings..106
26: H and its combinations...109

27: Diphthongs 114
28: All about X 120

Part Four Keyboard

Part Five Reading and writing practice

Introduction

Tabor shorthand is *contemporary shorthand*. It is a method of writing notes by hand to keep pace with the spoken word. It is a method of "pen shorthand" in contrast to "machine shorthand" where an electronic writing machine is used. Pen shorthand is more flexible and appropriate for normal note-taking. Machine shorthand is used particularly in legal court reporting.

Writing notes by hand is simple and fast at any time. This method of "notes by hand" is especially easy to learn and to write because it is derived from, and associated with, the familiar letters of your own script hand-writing.

It is a method of contemporary shorthand which uses simple letter forms and a minimum of abbreviation rules. It is an integrated system with a multilevel approach to writing the spoken word quickly. The system is designed to be written by all categories of people who need shorthand for taking notes.

For the convenience of students, this book is arranged in four parts:

Part One: **Fundamental principles** of the system. These apply throughout all levels and need to be studied first.

Each of the following Parts is a complete course in itself, but you need to decide which course is appropriate for you.

Part Two: **Basic mode,** the level used by professional shorthand writers and those who regularly need to make rapid verbatim notes. At this level simplified letters are used, all of which are derived from familiar longhand or print forms and written as single pen-strokes.

Part Three: **Alpha-script level,** for the general note-taker where very high writing speeds are not required. Familiar longhand letters are written instead of the simplified letters of Basic mode.

Part Four: **Keyboard,** a special version which can be used by touch-keyboarders who wish to make notes on an electronic QWERTY keyboard. It can be written as pen shorthand in its essential form.

The integrated approach enables two significant features to be applied, ***a common core of rules for word abbreviation*** and ***letter*** *simplification*. As a result of years of research this *common core of rules* has been reduced to a mere handful, but together they cover ways of writing the sounds of the English language.

The second feature, *letter simplification,* provides a progressive approach enabling everyone to use the system to meet personal needs and way of writing. All letters are derived from their familiar longhand or print equivalents and are easily written and recognized.

These features set this method apart from other shorthand systems.

Who should read this book

This book is intended for everyone who attends meetings and who writes some form of notes during the meeting. This includes

- ✓ business meetings, from Board-room to shop-floor
- ✓ professional meetings, both client / professional and peer groups
- ✓ meetings of associations and organizations
- ✓ conferences, workshops and seminars
- ✓ educational meetings, college, university and high-school classes

In the worlds of journalism, business and education, anyone who attends any kind of meeting will find that this shorthand method is an invaluable way of making quick notes or a record of the discussion for personal use.

The contemporary approach

This method of shorthand is a totally flexible system of writing. For those who take notes frequently, Basic-mode is used. This serves those who regularly need to write verbatim shorthand at speeds in excess of 100 words a minute such as professional journalists, reporters, secretaries and shorthand typists. For the occasional or general user, Alpha-script level enables anyone to more than double their normal speed of writing..

Many people create their own 'shorthand'; this is usually no more than a personal approach to abbreviating words. Such abbreviations contain many personal idiosyncrasies and are not intended for general use. This contemporary approach, however, is a total *system*, a consistent method of writing words and phrases quickly and accurately.

Although the theory can be learned in only a few hours of study, shorthand is essentially a writing skill and, like learning any skill, you will need to practise! Take every opportunity to write in shorthand; even if you do not have a pen and pencil with you, trace word outlines on your knee or against a book and mentally "write" words you hear or see on signs in shops or in the street. This will get you into the habit of thinking shorthand and will greatly help you to master the system.

This shorthand method is based on your normal handwriting but at the professional level each letter is simplified to a single pen-stroke which is easily recognized and quickly written. The basic principles of abbreviation deal with the most frequently occurring sounds; a few rules enable you to write any word quickly and accurately. You can proceed at your own pace to achieve whatever level of proficiency you wish. Achievement is literally in your own hands!

Approach to study

The system is presented progressively so that you can gradually build up your skills. The rules are few and simple but do take care that you thoroughly understand each point before moving on to the next. Don't merely read a rule; write out each example given several times and make sure that your brain, eye and hands work together to fix the rule and its application into your memory. The surest way to learn is to *say* each example word aloud, to *visualize* its consonant structure and then to *write* down the word outline neatly and accurately. Try to follow the sequence;

See it - Say it - Write it!

In order to get the most out of this course you should approach your study seriously. Practise writing shorthand regularly - use it every day until it becomes part of your life. The art of writing shorthand, once mastered, will be a valuable asset throughout your life.

When writing shorthand try to keep all letters and strokes a consistent size, not too small that they cannot be clearly recognized nor too large which wastes time. Write each outline quickly and evenly with a light pressure of the pen; never scribble an outline. There is no point in writing an outline rapidly if you cannot read it afterwards!

You can use pen or pencil and many writers use a fine ball-point pen which enables smooth and fast writing. A fountain pen with a fine flexible nib is an excellent writing tool. Pencils wear down quickly so always have several to hand, ready sharpened.

Arrangement of text

The text is arranged for easy learning with certain sections specially marked.

☑ This icon indicates a **Principal Rule** of the system with the text of the rule in bold print; some example words illustrate the principle.

✓ This indicates a General Guideline recommended to be followed.

✐ Occasionally a **Writing Tip** is given; these are indicated by the pen symbol. A writing tip does not have the force of a rule, but is a suggested way of writing arising from previous experience.

the Words printed in italics are Quick Forms; these are specially abbreviated forms for the most frequently occurring words.

Contemporary Shorthand

Part One
Fundamental principles

Roy B. Tabor

1: Writing the sound of words

Shorthand is a way of capturing the spoken word as a written record. This method is the contemporary approach to writing shorthand. Even with modern electronic technology, handwritten notes are still one of the best ways of recording notes; they are extremely flexible and easy to read and use afterwards.

What you are recording are the *sounds of speech*. Each word is reduced on paper to its basic sound structure.

☑ **Words are written according to the way they sound.**
In this system you hear a word and you write down the letters representing the sounds of that word. Thus 'knew' is written as *'nu'* and 'weigh' is written as *'wa'*; the sound of 'f' is always written as an 'f' whether it occurs as f, gh, or ph, in such words as face, stuff, tough, phase or photograph. In this way most words can be represented by a very short "outline" of consonants and significant vowels.

☑ **Each word 'outline' is formed using the sounded consonants and significant vowels.**
Mostly your notes will consist of sentences. The context of a sentence is an excellent guide to the meaning of individual words and this fact will allow you to write quite short word outlines which can be read back easily.

By way of demonstration, can you read the following sentences?

a oue iie aai ie ao a
o e o o o e a i e eio

Probably not! But, if we write them as,

'a hos dvdd agnst tslf cnt stnd,'
't b r nt t b, tht s e qstn'

you will easily read them as

"A house divided against itself cannot stand".

"To be or not to be, that is the question".

This illustrates the principle that it is the *consonant structure* of a word which gives the word 'picture' or 'outline'. In

Contemporary Shorthand

shorthand we write the consonants to represent a word with a few significant vowels for added clarity.

But merely leaving out a few vowels and silent letters does not make a useful abbreviation system. We need to follow a set of consistent rules whereby we can write any word quickly in a shortened form and one which can always be easily recognized. Clearly the consonant 'outline' is very important, but we also need a simple way to indicate the correct vowels in any word. In the next chapter you will learn the easy way to indicate vowels.

Roy B. Tabor

2: The vowel system

Vowel indicators

The *context of a sentence* usually gives a clear indication of the relevant vowels within a word. However, there are times when it will be necessary to indicate a vowel precisely. This may occur if you need to write isolated words or to label a diagram or to write names and addresses.

A simple but consistent system is used to indicate vowels. These simple signs are written as short diacritical marks; *they may be written upwards or downwards*, whichever is most convenient and distinctive.

☑ *The vowel indicators are*

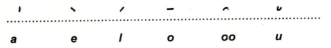

This is not intended to be a system of phonetics where all shades of vowel sounds are represented. The indicators are used as a general guide to the vowel. Thus the vowel sounds as heard in the words 'high', 'tie', and 'guide' are all represented by the 'i' indicator. Similarly the vowel sounds heard in the words 'few', 'true' and 'view' are all indicated by the 'u' indicator. The vowels used are essentially *indicators* and may be read and pronounced differently by local speakers as dialect or local custom. In practice this presents very few difficulties.

Vowels may generally be considered to be either short or long. The short vowels occur in the words 'back', 'get', 'kick', 'dog', 'book' and 'luck'. The long vowels occur in the words 'gate', 'meet', 'site', 'tone', 'food' and 'glue'.

✓ **Short vowels** are usually omitted in words forming phrases and sentences where the consonant structure is sufficient to indicate the meaning of each word. For words standing alone or where it may be helpful to write in a short

Contemporary Shorthand

vowel, the relevant indicator is placed **ABOVE** the word outline in the position where the vowel occurs;

✓ *The long vowels* are indicated by writing the same vowel indicator but placed **BELOW** the word outline.

It is important to remember that the consonant 'skeleton' of a word will give you an excellent indication of words written in context, that is, as part of a sentence. Students tend to use a lot of vowels at first, especially as in these early days many isolated example words are written. However, as you progress and begin to write more connected matter you will soon find yourself leaving out the unnecessary vowels. The great advantage of this contemporary method is that at any time you can use the vowel indicators to indicate vowels precisely.

(See also chapter 4 for further ways of writing vowels.)

✓ *On their own the vowel indicators also represent these words;*

```
  ı         `         ,         -         ◡
```

a, and   the   I   of   you

Punctuation

Normal punctuation signs may be used. However it is common practice to write a small 'x-cross' at the end of a sentence to indicate the period or full-stop; this can be modified to indicate a comma. It is not necessary to modify a colon or semi-colon, but if preferred these punctuation signs can be circled; a dash and curved brackets (parentheses) are crossed through,

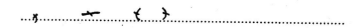

Proper nouns are usually indicated by writing two small lines below the word outline. (An alternative is to thicken the first letter of the word.)

Roy B. Tabor

Part Two
Basic Mode

Contemporary Shorthand

3: Writing consonants

The consonants

As you have seen earlier, the consonants give you the 'picture' of a word. However, this system is different from some earlier shorthand systems in that you are not required to learn an entirely new and unfamiliar alphabet of arbitrary signs to represent the consonants. In this method you use the familiar letters of your own hand-writing but we show you how these may be simplified for quick writing.

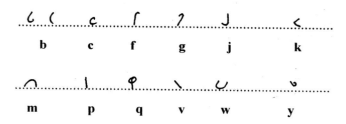

(See chapter 4 for ways of writing the alternative forms of B.)

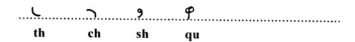

In a word outline each letter is written directly on to the preceding one without any joining strokes.

In this method of shorthand there is no mandatory right or wrong way to write a word outline; it can be tailored to individual requirements. The emphasis is on each person writing what is familiar; this aids initial learning, makes remembering easy and results in easily read outlines.

The sound of consonants

Shorthand is written according to the sound of the words you hear. The following notes include comments on those consonants which have hard and soft forms.

The letter 'c' is used for the hard 'k' sound which occurs in the words, *cup, cat, act, luck, back* and *kick.*

K is used to indicate initials; some writers prefer to write initials in ordinary longhand (but see chapter 12 for a specific use of K).

Note that the sound of 'f' may occur in different spellings as in the words, *fun, cliff, cough* and *photograph.*

The letter 'g' is used for the hard sound which occurs in the words, *go, gun, game, pig, log* and *dig.*

The letter 'j' is used for the soft 'g' sound which occurs in the words, *gin, jam, badge, dodge, wedge, jacket, gem* and *adjourn.*

'q' is found as a double sound, 'qu' (pronounced as 'kw'); it is given a very distinctive form.

Ways of writing 'x' are explored in chapter 14.

'y' is represented as a combination of the vowel indicators E + U when it occurs as a sounded consonant. As a *vowel* it may be sounded as 'ee', as in *happy* or as the diphthong 'i' as in *dry,* and for these the relevant vowel indicator is written.

The core consonants

The core consonants are the most frequently occurring letters and each of these is ***written in a simplified form derived from the longhand letter.*** They are a key feature of this shorthand method as together they form about half of the consonants in every sentence.

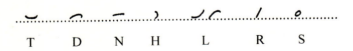

T　　D　　N　　H　　L　　R　　S

D is the initial stroke of the longhand letter *d.*
T is the final curved stroke of the longhand letter *t.*

Contemporary Shorthand

You may like to think of these signs as T, the lighter sound, which rises upwards, while D, the heavier sound, drops downwards.

(Ways of writing D and T are explored further in chapter 6).

N is a horizontal stroke, straight as a Nail from eNd - to - eNd.

H is usually lightly sounded and can often be omitted It is derived from the first part of the loop in the longhand letter; it is always written *downwards*.

('H' and its combinations, CH and SH, are explored in chapter 10).

L is derived from the upper loop of the longhand letter. Both forms are written *upwards*. (See chapter 9 for ways of writing L)

R is derived from the main stem of the longhand letter; it may be written either *upwards* or *downwards*.

(Ways of writing R are explored in chapter 7).

S is derived from the small circle formed at the top of the longhand letter. *'S stands for circle'*! It may be written *clock-wise* or *anti- clockwise*, whichever makes the easiest and most convenient join.

The S-circle may sometimes be written as a simple dot. At the end of a word this is a fast and simple way to indicate plurals.

The sound of Z is indicated by the S-circle preceded by a dot-identifier but this is rarely necessary.

Before you move on, do practise writing all the consonants given in this chapter. Write each letter several times; slowly and accurately at first and them write them quickly. Try to feel the movement needed to form each letter so that you can write all letters smoothly, accurately and, above all, consistently. They are *letters* to be written not signs to be drawn.

Roy B. Tabor

4: Writing the word outline

Writing words

Now that you have been introduced to the vowels and consonants you can begin to write words.

✓ *The first letter of the word outline normally rests on the line and each following letter begins where the preceding one ends.*

| bank | log | miss | win | gun | given |

It is important that each letter is formed clearly; don't scribble your letters as this will only lead to confusion. Get into the habit of writing precise letters at this stage and you will soon be able to write faster with practice. Remember that a word outline is essentially a skeleton of consonants with any significant vowels added for clarity.

The word outline is the *sound picture* of a word. Within the *context of a sentence* similar word outlines may represent different words; for example, 'gv' may represent *give* or *gave*.

✓ *Short vowels are omitted in the body of a word.*

✓ *Initial short vowels are usually included in the outline.*

an initial vowel indicator is joined on, or written close, to the start of the first consonant.

✓ *A final vowel is written on the line following the final consonant;* it is usually disjoined.

| aid | age | echo | egg | in | on | open |

Contemporary Shorthand

pay	gay	die	tie	day

✒ The vowel indicator is joined to a preceding S-circle.

say	see, sea	sigh	so	sue

✒ The fast way to write long vowels is to join the indicator on to the last consonant of the word. This is a positive indication that you must read the vowel *in the body of the word*, and not as a final vowel.

lane	line	sign	take	pain	tone	tune

✒ Occasionally, and where appropriate, a long vowel indicator may be used as a joining stroke in the middle of a word.

rain	safe	pipe	cake	nine

✒ When a long vowel precedes a final S the S-circle is usually written first followed by the appropriate vowel sign.

case	pace	peace	lease	mice	dose

But the S-circle is usually written *after* U or OO.

ruse	fuse	moose	loose

✓ *The OO indicator may be used as an alternative for O where it makes an easier join.*

own	phone	know

11

Roy B. Tabor

At first you are likely to use many indicators as you write stand-alone words. Once you become more familiar with the system you will soon discover that the short vowel indicators may be omitted when writing sentences.

Alternative B

The alternative forms for B are provided to enable easy joins; the full form is used particularly before T, L and N; the short form is used particularly before C, D, F and M.

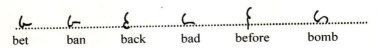

bet   ban   back   bad   before   bomb

Practice 1

Write out the following examples several times. Remember, the more practice you have in writing shorthand the more fluent you will become.

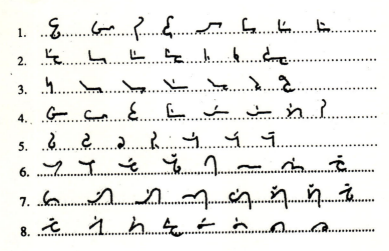

1. cab, bone, gap, fake, line, fine, pin, pen,
2. pink, pain, pan, panic, pay, peace/ piece, picnic,

Contemporary Shorthand

3. pipe, vein / vain, vine, van, venue, view, civic.
4. ban, cone, back, fan, tin, tan, ham, hip,
5. hub, hack, his, happy, tap, tip, top,
6. tug, tough, tick, tub, map, done, mad, dock,
7. bad, limp, lamp, damp, camp, hump, pump, rob,
8. rock, rap, ram, rank, sin, sad, some, miss.

Roy B. Tabor

5: Quick forms

Frequently occurring words

There are a number of commonly occurring words some of which are given special Quick Forms, much as you abbreviate such words as – *road **rd**, amount **amt**,* and *avenue **ave**,* in normal writing. They are given special attention because they occur so frequently. You probably use some of these abbreviated words already when you write notes. In this text these words are printed in *italics*.

Shorthand is a writing skill and with regular and constant use you will soon find that the word outlines become very familiar and that you are writing them easily and quickly. It will not be long before you find yourself writing words automatically as you hear them spoken.

These most frequently occurring words are presented in two groups. To start with, there is a small number of very important words which are among those most frequently heard in everyday speech. Together these few words form about a quarter of all spoken and written language. They should therefore be learned thoroughly and used often. Fortunately they are easily written and remembered.

Group 1 Quick Forms

a, an, and	*the*	*be, by, but*	*do*	*have, very*	*no, not*

I, why	*is*	*of*	*it, to*	*at*	*in*	*on*	*we, with*

The next group of words is equally important, as altogether the two groups make up almost half of all written matter. By learning and using these words you will be able to write some fifty per cent of everything you will ever need. Use them as often as you can and they will soon become familiar friends.

Contemporary Shorthand

Group 2 Quick Forms

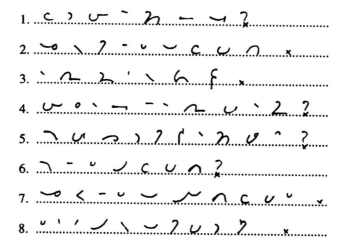

Practice 2

1. Can he win the game in time?
2. It is very good of you to come with me.
3. The man had a very bad cough.
4. What is the name of the man with the gun?
5. Which way did he go after the game was over?
6. Which of you will come with me?
7. It is kind of you to let me come with you.
8. You and I will have to go with him again.

Roy B. Tabor

6: Writing T and D

Writing T and D

The letters T and D are particularly important as so often they form part of the past tense of verbs. You will find that they occur in every sentence so you will get plenty of practice in writing them. Note that T, the lighter sound, curves upward, while D, the heavier sound, curves downward.

☑ *T is written as an anti-clockwise curve, and D is written as a clock-wise curve.*

(	⌣	⌣	⌣	⌒	⌒	⌒	⌒
bet	took	wet	sat	deaf	fed	mad	had

✓ *When T follows or precedes N it is modified to a small hook;*
this is always written anti-clockwise;

| bent | want | meant | paint | tent | attain |

When writing the **STN combination** the use of the T-hook + N is optional. You may prefer to write S + T + N, both are permissible, but using the T-hook is faster to write.

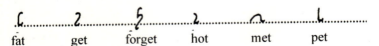

| stand | stunt | instant | distance |

The T-hook may be used after the downward letters, F, G, H, M, P.

(	2	5	2	⌒	(
fat	get	forget	hot	met	pet

Contemporary Shorthand

☑ *Similarly, D is written as a clockwise hook following N;*

| bend | send | find | end | hand | attend | wind |

Writing D

The D-hook may also be used whenever it is found to be more convenient, particularly after L, W, and R.

| sold | filed | red | rodent | would | widow |

When the sounds of T and D follow each other they are written as a continuous double curve;

| wanted | scented | rotted | debt | hunted |

At the beginning of a word the D hook may be written before J, L, P and V to make an easy join.

| digit | delete | done | depend | devalue |

Practice 3

1.

2.

3.

4.

5.

6.

1. I meant to send the pen back to you.
2. It was good of you to lend me the pen.
3. I do not want you to send him away.
4. He wanted to put the money in the bank.
5. He took the weapon from the dead man.
6. At the end of the day we will get what we want.

Writing TH

☑ *TH is indicated by writing T at a downward slope.*
The TH-stroke represents the words, *than*, *thank* and *thing*..

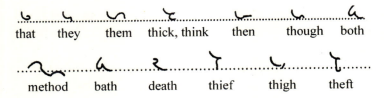

Here are some useful combination words with '**thing**'.

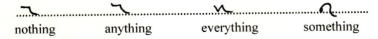

Practice 4

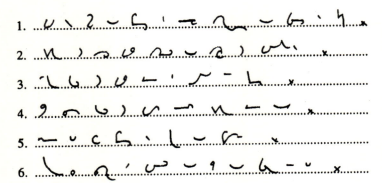

Contemporary Shorthand

1. We have got to find a new method to bend the pipe.
2. Everything he did was meant to make him wealthy.
3. I think that he was in a lot of pain.
4. She said that he would know everything in time.
5. Only you can find the path to follow.
6. There is something I want to say to both of you.

Writing syllable T and D

✓ *A normal T or D is written to indicate a T or D syllable.*

By writing the full letter instead of a modified hook form we indicate that a long vowel intervenes.

The relevant vowel indicator may be included, joined on to the final letter, but this is not usually needed when writing connected matter where the context is the guide to the meaning of the word.

| feet | gate | light | boat | wait, weight | meet, meat |

| fade | deed | wide | load | food | made | hide |

✓ *Alternative forms*

Writers of Alpha-level may wish to continue to indicate a final syllable T or D by writing the relevant superscript vowel indicator (see Chapter 22). This indicates the vowel precisely but because it involves a small jump of the pen to write the disjoined indicator it is slightly slower than writing the full form T or D; a D may be added to the superscript vowel indicator to form a past participle. The following examples demonstrate these alternatives.

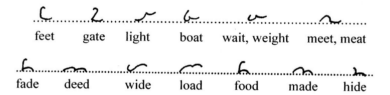

| state | beat | white | fade | deed | side |
| stated | heated | waited | faded | guided | coded |

Notice that a final long vowel is always written on the line beside the final consonant, whereas the syllable T and D vowel indicators are written clearly *above the line in the superscript position*. Compare the following,

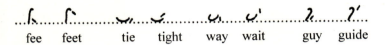

fee   feet   tie   tight   way wait   guy   guide

A following '-st' is indicated by adding the S-circle. The following examples also show the alternative use of a vowel indicator.

neatest   latest   tightest   widest

The word ending '**-uate**' is represented by U + T. This may be written either as UT (T) or as a superscript U vowel indicator + A.

insinuate   actuate   punctuate

CN and CT blends

When N or T follows C, the two letters are blended into a single stroke. Note that the 'tail' of the C is the part that is modified; the C is always begun in the normal position.

candid   cancel   canvas   act   tact   fact

(See also chapter 8 for the CV blend.)

Contemporary Shorthand

Practice 5

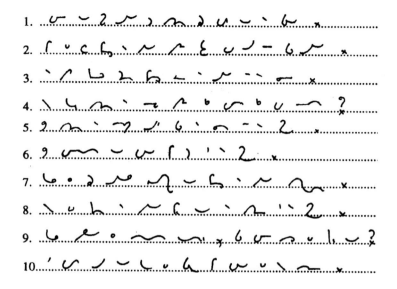

1. When it got light he made his way to the boat.
2. If you can find the right road back we will not be late.
3. The red paint had faded in the light of the sun.
4. Have they made the new road as wide as we need?
5. She made the dog lie by the side of the gate.
6. She wanted to wait for him at the gate.
7. This is his latest attempt to find the right method.
8. Have you paid the right fee to the man at the gate?
9. This receipt is dated today, but when did you pay it?
10. I would like to thank you both for what you have done.

Roy B. Tabor

7: The sound of R

Consonant R

☑ *R is read after any consonant which is doubled in size.*

| drink | drug | drum | tree | try | truth | trade |

| bread | cry | free | grin | pride | prison |

Syllable R

Following the rule that short vowels are omitted in the body of a word, a double size letter may also indicate an *R-syllable,* i.e., where there is an intervening vowel.

Where necessary the relevant short vowel indicator can be written above the word outline. In practice you will find it rarely necessary to insert a short vowel indicator when the words occur in connected matter; the context of the sentence will almost always indicate the precise meaning.

The following examples illustrate this principle.

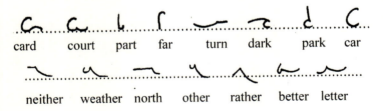

| card | court | part | far | turn | dark | park | car |

| neither | weather | north | other | rather | better | letter |

Where the intervening vowel is LONG, the R is usually written.

Contemporary Shorthand

care	pair	near	fair	dear	here

The R is written where *it is sounded separately,* or, *if it makes a more compact outline.* It is always written after S, V and W.

derive	hurry	ferry	craft	crop	fragrant

serve	sort	never	cover	warden	were

The R is written following an initial vowel indicator.

art	argue	arrive	erect	iron	urge	your

urban	urgent	earth	earned	order	organ

The R itself may be doubled in length to add a following R sound.

rare	rear	error	roar	uproar

When R follows the ND blend it is often easier to write an upward R rather than a double-length D.

wander	sender	binder	finder	thunder

Writing PR

The upward R may be used with P to indicate **syllable PR**; but a double-length P may sometimes be more convenient.

compare	repair	approve	despair	purpose

depart   report   support   permit   permanent   pursue

✓ An initial **consonant PR** may be indicated by ***writing a normal length P in the superscript position*** (i.e. where you would begin a double-length P). This is used particularly for the prefixes PRE- and PRO-. A double-length P may be written where it is more convenient.

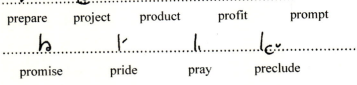

prepare   project   product   profit   prompt

promise   pride   pray   preclude

When PR is followed by V the double-length P is merged with the V and is written on a slant.

prevent   prevalent   private   provide   province

A separate R is used with P to represent the prefix ***'para-'***.

paraffin   parasite   paratrooper   paramedic

The Quick Form for ***'for'*** is the letter F, and this is used for words beginning with the word 'for'.

forgive   forget   fortune   forgotten   forgot

Note that there is a Quick Form for ***'ever'*** and ***'every'***, VR, which is used in the following combinations;

Contemporary Shorthand

everyone   everybody   every time   every way

Practice 6

1. He would rather part with his wife than give away his car.
2. Only here can we breathe pure air and be healthy.
3. She tried to park the car at-the far end of-the car-park.
4. The farmer had warned that-the fire in the barn might burn all night.
5. It was too dark to-go-on so they decided to make camp.
6. It was perfect weather for what they wanted to-do.
7. I can forgive you for everything you have done.
8. There was nothing he could have done to prevent the fire.
9. I can forgive, but never forget, what you have done.
10. Will they permit the parade to go forward today?

Writing 'than'

'Comparison' words such as 'better', 'wetter', and 'bigger' are usually followed by 'than'; these phrases are easily written.

nearer than   more than   quicker than   rather than

Word ending '-ly' and '-ty'

The word ending, *'-ly'* is indicated by writing the E-vowel at the end of the outline and *just below the line*. A final *'-ty'* may be indicated by writing the E-vowel *on the line*, but a T + E may often be more convenient.

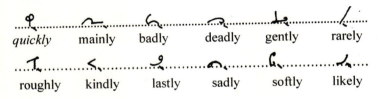

quickly   mainly   badly   deadly   gently   rarely

roughly   kindly   lastly   sadly   softly   likely

Compare the following outlines,

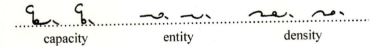

capacity   entity   density

Practice 7

1.
2.
3.
4.
5.

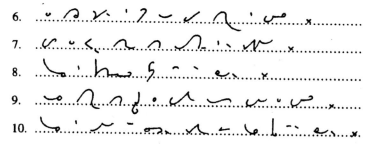

1. The car was more than he could afford.
2. Would you prefer to meet at eight rather than seven.
3. We heard that the car was badly in need of repair.
4. She tried to park her car nearer to the gate of the market.
5. The majority seemed to live in dire poverty.
6. You must hurry and go to your mother at once.
7. Would you kindly meet me tomorrow at the airport.
8. There is a permanent fog over the city.
9. It is more than my job is worth to do what you want.
10. There is a lot of sandy earth in this part of the city.

Roy B. Tabor

8: The sounds of S and Z

Writing S and Z

The sounds of S and Z are the most commonly occurring sounds in the English language. S occurs in every sentence and it is a principal indicator of plural words. Because of this high frequency it deserves special attention.

☑ *The simplified letter for S is a small circle; this is derived from the upper part of the longhand letter.*

| sad | said | same | send | save | say | second |

| sense | set | sign | snow | step | certain | reserve |

The S-circle provides an easy join between two letters and it can be tucked into a preceding or following letter in a single smooth movement of the pen.

| concern | service | resign | reside | escape | visit |

| lesson | missed | receive | easy | pass | business |

✓ *After P the S-circle is always written counter-clockwise* to distinguish it from J+S where it is written *clockwise*.

| pass | passed | justice | justly |

Contemporary Shorthand

Indicating Z

☑ *The sound of Z is indicated by the S-circle preceded by a dot identifier when necessary.*

| laser | jazz | zero | craze | freeze | blaze |

The sounds of S and Z are so similar that in practice there is rarely a need to mark it separately.

Plural S

Where a final S represents a plural word the S-circle may be reduced to a simple S-dot. It is used to indicate the plural of any abbreviated word.

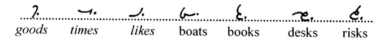

| goods | times | likes | boats | books | desks | risks |

✎ Use the S-dot as convenient, to indicate a final 's' sound;

| fights | dates | beats | caters | comes | fighters |

The S-dot is also used with a vowel indicator when it represents a syllable T or D.

| dates | rates | beats | fights | sights | coats |

Practice 8

1.
2.
3.
4.
5.
6.
7.

    1. speak, step, spend, stick, sun, some, say, justice, sip
    2. see, send, sack, sink, guess, miss, was, passage, spot,
    3. cross, use, less, press, this, these, nice, passed, spin,
    4. niece, wise, revise, space, police, spend, times,
    5. sick, stand, something, sent, Sabbath, succeed, case,
    6. face, peace, his, caress, depress, fences, dances, dims,
    7. comes, trees, froze, laser, Senate, passive, beats, western.

Double 'ses'

The double 'ses' sound as heard in 'crisis' and 'sister', is indicated by writing a disjoined S-circle.

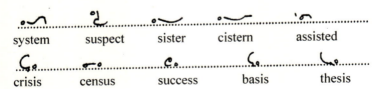

system   suspect   sister   cistern   assisted

crisis   census   success   basis   thesis

The plural S-dot is used in the normal way after a word ending in S.

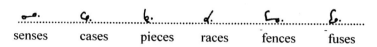

senses　　cases　　pieces　　races　　fences　　fuses

Final '-st'

The final T may be omitted in words ending in '-st'.

just　　past　　west　　must　　insist　　persist

The prefixes 'con-' and 'com-'

Many words begin with this general prefix which may occur as **con-, com-, cam-** or **cum-**. All these prefixes are represented by the letter 'c'. (The 'c' may be disjoined for **com-** if preferred.)

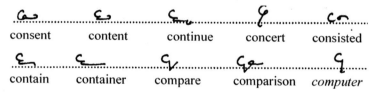

consent　　content　　continue　　concert　　consisted

contain　　container　　compare　　comparison　　*computer*

The prefixes *'can-' and 'coun-'* are represented by writing 'c + n'.

candid　　cancer　　candy　　count　　counter　　county

CV blend

When V follows the prefix 'con-' the C and V are blended together.

Note that the C is always begun in its normal position and its' 'tail' only is modified.

convict　　convey　　converse　　convenient

31

Roy B. Tabor

Practice 9

1.
2.
3.
4.
5.
6.
7.
8.
9.
10.

1. It-was sad that he-had to sell his business so quickly.
2. We must insist that you will pursue this case to a just end.
3. It-is easy to miss your way unless you can read a map.
4. In some sense it could be said that she has second sight.
5. The sun sets in-the west every night.
6. I suspect that it was his sister took the jar of jam.
7. We continue to have great success every year.
8. He has a good system which is the basis of his success.
9. She would like you to assist her to prepare the concert.
10. They were content to continue as they had begun.

Contemporary Shorthand

9: The sound of L

Writing L

The letter L has two forms; both curves are derived from the loop of the longhand letter. They are both written *upwards.* Use whichever form creates the best join with the adjacent letters.

line	lip	alone	life	luck	lid	lie

left	leg	less	let	live	listen

Syllable L

L may be written to indicate an L syllable; any long vowel is usually omitted.

careful	useful	double	trouble	couple	formal

file	pile	mile	coal	deal	goal

It would also be permissible to write these last examples by writing the relevant vowel indicator below the line, in the L-position. (See the following section.)

Note how the following words may be written.

usual	usually	unusual	unusually

Roy B. Tabor

The L position

Following a consonant, the sound of L may indicated by writing a letter through or below the line; this is the L-position.

✓ *A **final L syllable*** is indicated by writing the preceding letter disjoined and through or below the line.

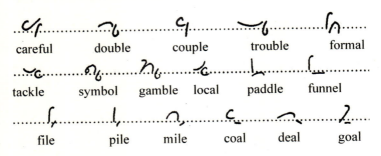

✓ Where the intervening vowel is **short**, ***the whole outline may be written through or below the line.*** When the L letter is written, it is a positive indication that the intervening vowel is **long**.

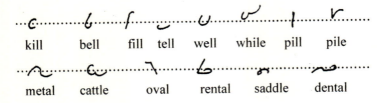

Word endings '-ual', '-ule' and '-ulate'

The word endings '-ual' and '-ule' may be indicated by writing the U-vowel indicator through or below the line, in the subscript position. The letter L may be written if preferred.

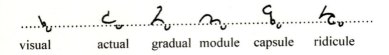

Alternatively you could write these words with a final L.

visual	actual	gradual	module	capsule	ridicule

The word ending '-ulate' is indicated by writing a subscript U + A or alternatively, L + T, as preferred.

speculate	regulate	stimulate	tabulate	postulate

or,

speculate	regulate	stimulate	tabulate	postulate

Consonant L

The same principle of the L-position can also be applied in the L-consonant combinations. Some writers may prefer to write in the L, but the following tactic can be a valuable contribution to increased writing speeds.

✓ *L may be omitted when it occurs in the consonant combinations, BL, CL, FL, GL and PL; the preceding letter is written through the line.* (The L-position.)

The first letter of the combination is written only partly through the line in order to keep the pen as close to the line of writing as possible. Any prefix letter may be written normally above the line.

black	blind	climb	glad	pleasure

35

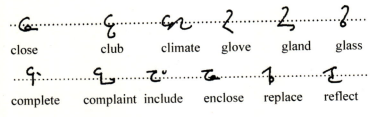

Note that SL is always written as S + L on the line.

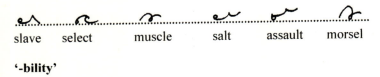

'-bility'

The word ending '**-bility**' is simply indicated by writing a disjoined B + E through the line.

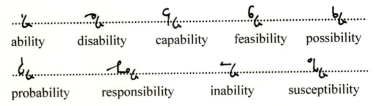

Words incorporating the **'al-'** (all) syllable are indicated by writing a clock-wise L.

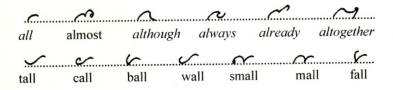

Contemporary Shorthand

Practice 10

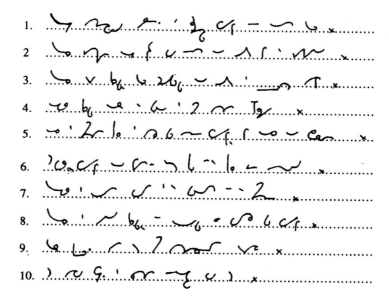

1. There are medical reasons why he-should-be careful not to-do that.
2. There-is ample time before we need to leave for the airport.
3. There-is every possibility that he-will-be-able to live a normal life.
4. It-was possible to-see the boat a good mile off-shore.
5. It is a gradual process and must be done carefully if it is to succeed.
6. He was careful to follow each part of the process in detail.
7. There was a tall wall at the bottom of the garden.
8. There is a real possibility of trouble so we must be careful.
9. These plants all have great medicinal value.
10. He always carries a small notebook with him.

Roy B. Tabor

10: H and its combinations

Writing H

H is often very lightly sounded when it occurs at the beginning of a word and in such cases it can often be omitted. Note the Quick Form for *'who'* and *'whom'* where the vowel indicator is written on its side to distinguish it from *'you'*.

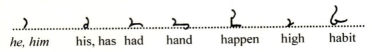

| home | who, whom | hope | higher | huge | whose |

☑ *The simplified letter for H is a short right-handed curve, this is derived from the upper loop of the longhand letter, it is always written downwards.*

| he, him | his, has | had | hand | happen | high | habit |

Note the differences in writing the following frequent word groups.

| has, his | he is | he's | he says |

When R follows H, a double length H is used following the general rule that letters are doubled in size to indicate the addition of R. However, as usual, the R is written when it is sounded separately or when a long vowel intervenes.

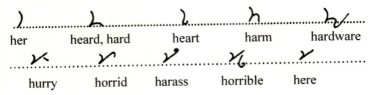

| her | heard, hard | heart | harm | hardware |
| hurry | horrid | harass | horrible | here |

Contemporary Shorthand

Double consonants with H; CH, SH.

The double consonants formed with H are TH, CH and SH. You have already been introduced to TH which is a T written at a slant.

Similarly CH is represented by writing an H at a slant.

SH is represented by combining the two letters S and H.

Writing CH

☑ *CH is represented by writing H on a downward slant.*

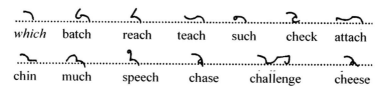

| which | batch | reach | teach | such | check | attach |
| chin | much | speech | chase | challenge | cheese |

A following R sound is usually indicated by adding an upward R; but a double-length CH may sometimes be more convenient to write.

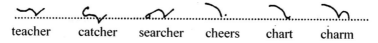

teacher   catcher   searcher   cheers   chart   charm

Writing SH

☑ *SH is written by combining S and H.*

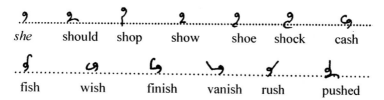

| she | should | shop | show | shoe | shock | cash |
| fish | wish | finish | vanish | rush | pushed |

R is added to SH by writing an upward R. It is not incorrect to write a double-length SH (S + HR) but writing the R usually makes a more compact outline.

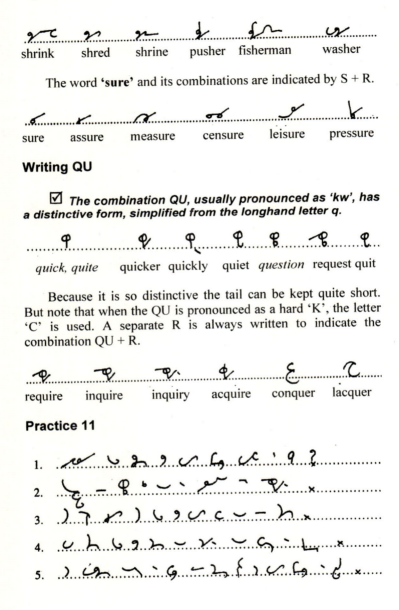

shrink shred shrine pusher fisherman washer

The word **'sure'** and its combinations are indicated by S + R.

sure assure measure censure leisure pressure

Writing QU

☑ *The combination QU, usually pronounced as 'kw', has a distinctive form, simplified from the longhand letter q.*

quick, quite quicker quickly quiet *question* request quit

Because it is so distinctive the tail can be kept quite short. But note that when the QU is pronounced as a hard 'K', the letter 'C' is used. A separate R is always written to indicate the combination QU + R.

require inquire inquiry acquire conquer lacquer

Practice 11

1.
2.
3.
4.
5.

Contemporary Shorthand

6. [shorthand]
7. [shorthand]
8. [shorthand]
9. [shorthand]
10. [shorthand]

1. Are you sure that she-said she would finish work at nine?
2. There-can-be no question as to the result of-the inquiry.
3. Her chief assured her that she would come to no harm.
4. We heard that she had to hurry to catch the plane.
5. He wished to-have the cash in hand before he would finish the job.
6. I am sure that she will come to no harm in your shop.
7. After his speech she had several questions to ask him.
8. Can you assure her that you will pay cash for the shoes?
9. They did not know whose request should be dealt with first.
10. Give us the tools and we will finish the job.

Roy B. Tabor

11: The sound of 'shun'

The 'shun' ending

The word ending pronounced '*shun*', occurs frequently; it is spelled variously as '-tion', '-sion' and '-cian'. For many years it has been an accepted convention among writers and printers to shorten these endings to a small 'n' written at the end of the word above the line.

Here we continue this practice.

☑ *The 'shun' ending is indicated by writing a disjoined* **N.**

direction	mention	operation	action	description

Keep this close to the last letter of the word and above the line. It is not usually necessary to insert the preceding vowel indicator as the context will normally give the meaning of the word. However, a preceding vowel indicator may be included if needed.

station	occasion	location	edition	quotation

condition	reservation	corporation	tension	ocean

attention	fashion	motion	nation	session

The plural of these words is indicated by writing a final S-dot.

When L follows the shun-ending, as in '**-tional**', the shun-N is written below the line (the L position).

42

Contemporary Shorthand

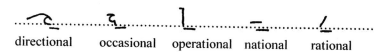

| directional | occasional | operational | national | rational |

The shun -N is doubled in length in the usual way to indicate the addition of a following R sound.

| practitioner | pensioner | petitioner | conditioner |

The 'shunt' ending

☑ *The word ending pronounced 'shunt' and spelled as '-cient' or '-tient' is indicated by the Shun-N + T-hook.*
'-ciently' is similarly indicated with the addition of -LY, and '-ciency' by Shun-N + SE.

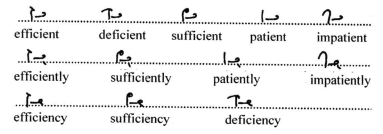

| efficient | deficient | sufficient | patient | impatient |

| efficiently | sufficiently | patiently | impatiently |

| efficiency | sufficiency | deficiency |

The 'shul' ending

There is an associated word ending which is pronounced as *'shul'* and spelled usually as **'-cial'**; this is indicated by writing a disjoined SH through the line; in practice it is usually shortened to H as a speed tactic.

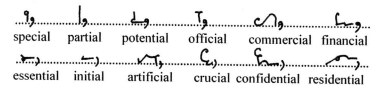

| special | partial | potential | official | commercial | financial |

| essential | initial | artificial | crucial | confidential | residential |

Roy B. Tabor

Practice 12

1.

2.

3.

4.

5.

6.

7.

8.

9.

10.

1. What action did you take initially?
2. That-is the direction she took to drive to-the station.
3. He only takes an occasional drink in order to-be social.
4. The official description is that-it-was a successful operation.
5. You must be both rational and patient in-this situation.
6. It is essential to be patient and then you can succeed.
7. This is a very special occasion for all of us.
8. We have made a reservation for you on the first possible flight.
9. They will approve your quotation on condition that you can deliver the goods on time.
10. On this occasion we suggest that you take *immediate* action.

Contemporary Shorthand

12: Vowels and Diphthongs

Writing AW

The sound of AW has a number of different spellings and it is pronounced variously in different parts of the country. It may occur as *'ought'*, *bought'*, *'taught'* or *'saw'*. It has a distinctive form as a combination of the vowel indicators for O + U; it is written as a thin or narrow letter 'o'.

In normal speech this is also heard in such words as *haul, hall, fall* and *tall,* and again in *law, saw* and *awesome.* Because shorthand is written according to the sound of words, and allowing for geographical variants in pronunciation, we can use the same vowel for all these words.

☑ **The sound of AW is indicated by a narrow or thin loop.**

ought	bought	fought	caught	taught	naughty

saw	law	jaw	awful	awesome	pawn

Writing '-alk'

The word ending '**-alk**' is represented by clockwise LC. (Alternatively the letter K may be used.)

talk	walk	walked	chalk	balk

The prefix '**auto-**' is indicated by AW; this may be disjoined.

automobile	autocrat	automated	auto

45

Roy B. Tabor

Diphthongs 'ow' and 'oi'

These diphthongs are combinations of two vowel sounds pronounced as a single syllable. Each has its own distinctive indicator.

☑ *OW is indicated by the longhand letter O.*

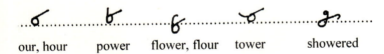

about	how	town	down	doubt	however
now	found	sound	allow	brown	round
house	mouse	outfit	outcome	output	outline

The sound of R is added to OW by adding an upward R.

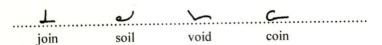

| our, hour | power | flower, flour | tower | showered |

☑ *OI is indicated by a crossed AW;* that is, the AW and E-vowel signs are combined.

| boy | coin | annoy | envoy | noise | oil |

Sometimes the OI indicator may be omitted for common words which are written in the context of a sentence.

| join | soil | void | coin |

46

Contemporary Shorthand

The crossed AW may be omitted in the following words.

employ employment employee unemployed

'en-, in-, un-'

For words beginning with 'en-' or 'in-', the initial vowel indicator is usually omitted. These prefixes occur very often and so, literally at a stroke, you can add a significant number of words to your shorthand vocabulary.

enough enter inform invade instead intend

Alternatively, the prefix '*in-*' may be indicated by writing only the *I-vowel indicator*. This is used mainly before D or H.

indefinite indicate induction inherit inherent

The prefix '*un-*' is usually represented by the *U-indicator written on the line.*

unable unlike unusual unless until

Roy B. Tabor

Practice 13

1.
2.
3.
4.
5.
6.
7.
8.
9.
10.

1. Her diction teacher used to say 'How now brown cow'.
2. He phoned her every hour on the hour.
3. It is time that we thought about the possible outcome of this action.
4. The entire crowd outside the house shouted with joy.
5. It was unusual, but not unknown, to-get such an official response.
6. You ought to talk to his daughter about her part in this matter.
7. There was a loud noise outside the house.
8. We-were always taught to behave properly at table.
9. She-said that she always bought her shoes down-town.
10. May we join you for your walk into town?

Contemporary Shorthand

13: The '-ng' ending

Writing the '-ng' ending

This word ending occurs frequently as '-ing' and forms the present participle of verbs, eg., *writing, eating, drinking, sleeping*. But it also occurs in such words as *long, sung, hang* and *belong*.

✓ *-NG is represented by writing a half-size G.* This is usually disjoined but it may be written on to the preceding consonant where convenient.

seeing   eating   drinking   sending   meeting   during

thanking   owing   landing   sitting   following   borrowing

song   belong   hang   lung   length

Because the NG indicator cannot be doubled in size, the sound of R is added to this suffix by writing the R-stroke.

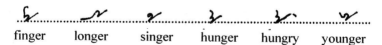

finger   longer   singer   hunger   hungry   younger

✓ When the NG- ending is itself followed by '-ing' it may be disjoined and written above the line, in the superscript position.

hanging   singing   belonging   ringing   longing   bringing

Roy B. Tabor

When an **L-syllable** is formed with NG, it is written in the L-position through or below the line.

jungle   shingle   angle   triangle   mingle   rectangle

The NG may also be used at the beginning of a word preceded by the relevant vowel indicator;

anger   angry   angler   England   English

But note that NG is not used in those words where the hard or soft G is pronounced;

angel   engage   engine   ingest   hinge   engineer

'-ment' and '-mount'

Both these word endings, **'-ment' and '-mount'** are represented by the letter M.

comment   document   element   moment   treatment   amount

This suffix becomes **'-mental'** by writing the M through the line in the L position.

fundamental   elemental   departmental

'-tive'

The word ending **'-tive'** is simply represented by the letter V.

comparative   competitive   motive   active   effective   relative

Practice 14

1.
2.
3.
4.
5.
6.
7.
8.
9.
10.

1. They continued eating and drinking all night.
2. The singer needed treatment for her sore throat.
3. I-am-sure that this time the treatment will-be effective.
4. For a moment I thought I-was seeing double.
5. The following comments should be noted.
6. It-is said that seeing is believing; now I-have seen, I believe.
7. The *chairman* said that he-had no comment to make to the press.

Roy B. Tabor

8. There-was a fundamental flaw in his argument.
9. We-have no effective treatment for this cancer at this moment.
10. Seeing all that eating and drinking on screen makes me feel hungry.

Contemporary Shorthand

14: All about X

Writing X

✓ *The sound of X is indicated by C + S* (pronounced 'ecks').

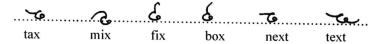

tax   mix   fix   box   next   text

[Because the letter X is so familiar some writers prefer to use the Alpha-level technique of writing a longhand 'x'. This may sometimes be simply and quickly indicated by writing a stroke across the preceding consonant;

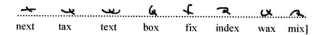

next   tax   text   box   fix   index   wax   mix]

Writing 'ex-'

The prefix **'ex-'** is one you will meet very often; it *is expressed by*
E + S. This is an abbreviation of E + C + S - "ecks".

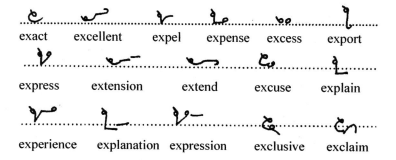

exact   excellent   expel   expense   excess   export

express   extension   extend   excuse   explain

experience   explanation   expression   exclusive   exclaim

53

Roy B. Tabor

Writing 'acc-' and 'ox-'

Initial '**acc-**' is indicated similarly by writing A + S.

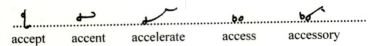

accept   accent   accelerate   access   accessory

The prefix '**ox-**' is similarly written as O + S.

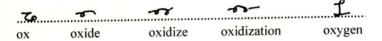

ox   oxide   oxidize   oxidization   oxygen

Practice 15

1.
2.
3.
4.
5.
6.
7.
8.
9.
10.

    1. It-is impossible to-be sure of-the exact amount he owes.
    2. To what extent did the jury believe the evidence?

Contemporary Shorthand

3. There-can-be no excuse for his actions in-this affair.
4. An index is a most important element in a book.
5. Jogging is usually regarded as an excellent form of exercise.
6. You will be expected to explain your actions to the meeting.
7. He is an expert and has considerable professional experience.
8. This is an excellent start to the project but an extension of time may be needed.
9. We wish to express our gratitude to you for all your help.
10. We-will-not accept any exclusions on access to the documentation.

Days and months

You will need to become familiar with writing the days and months and with expressing time. Mostly these are similar to the longhand abbreviations which you already use everyday so they should not present any difficulties. Notice how the word '*day*' can be expressed effectively by using the A-vowel indicator (but often even this can be omitted). Note that in the following examples the proper noun indicator is omitted for clarity.

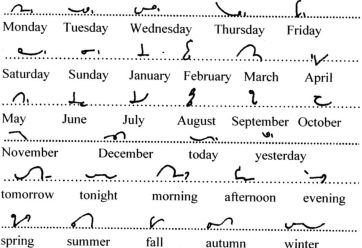

Roy B. Tabor

Practice 16

1. There-are thirty days in April, June and November.
2. Let me take you to dinner tomorrow evening.
3. The next meeting will-be held on Friday morning.
4. The deadline was agreed for the last Monday in May.
5. Yesterday I-was certain but to-day I-am-not so sure.
6. I would like to talk with you before the meeting on Wednesday.
7. It can be chilly on a wet November morning.
8. Tomorrow is another day, but tonight is for loving.
9. Today is the first day of the rest of your life.
10. We are expecting you tomorrow evening for dinner at eight.

Contemporary Shorthand

15: Double vowels

Double vowels

In a few words you will find that two vowels follow each other without forming a diphthong and so are sounded separately, eg. *create, radio, science* and *area*. Usually such words can be written following the general rules given, that is, by writing the stressed vowel and omitting the unstressed (short) vowel.

diet   poem   science   period   riot

☑ *The vowel combinations 'ea' or 'io' are indicated by combining the relevant indicators; 'ea' or 'io'.*

✎ In practice these are written as a small V, or an inverted V; they are written the same size as other vowel indicators. You may use either form as convenient.

area   idea   urea   radio   folio   polio

The sound of final L may be added to this combination double vowel by writing the combination *below the line* to indicate the word endings '-ial' or '-eal'.

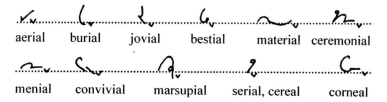

aerial   burial   jovial   bestial   material   ceremonial

menial   convivial   marsupial   serial, cereal   corneal

The word ending '**-iate**' can be simply indicated by writing the 'ia' combination vowel in the superscript position.

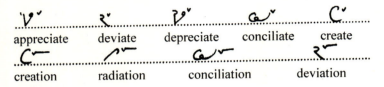

Practice 17

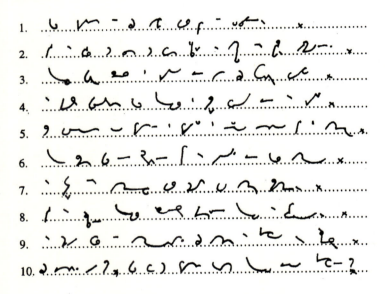

1. That period of his life was full of uncertainty.
2. After the *accident* he said he could appreciate the *importance* of the safety regulations.
3. There is both science and art in all his creative work.
4. The police believed that there was a serial killer in the area.
5. She wanted to follow a fruit and nut diet for a month.
6. There should be no deviation from the rules in this matter.

Contemporary Shorthand

7. The burial of the monarch was held with much ceremonial.
8. After the explosion there was extensive radiation through the factory.
9. The higher cost of materials has made the product very expensive.
10. His ideas are good, but can he follow them through into production?

Initial vowels

In most cases an initial vowel is joined to the following letter, but it may sometimes be necessary to disjoin the sign to make it more distinctive.

| adjust | adjacent | adjective | admit | adventure | adverb |

| appeal | approve | appear | apparent | abortion |

| icon | iron | operate | option | oval |

Initial 'ad-', 'ev-' and 'ob-'

You have already been introduced to the use of the I-indicator to indicate an initial prefix 'in-', and the U-indicator, often disjoined, is used to represent the prefix 'un-'. We now take this usage further with the other vowel indicators to represent initial prefixes.

A *disjoined A-vowel* may also indicate an initial '**ab-, ad-** or **av-**'

| admit | adjust | adopt | abandon | absolute | avenue |

Roy B. Tabor

A *disjoined E-vowel* may indicate an initial 'ev-'

evade	even	event	evolution	eventual

Similarly a *disjoined O vowel* indicates initial 'ob-' when it is followed by a consonant.

object	observe	obstruct	*BUT* obey	obese

Initial 'im-' and 'em-'

In words beginning with **'im-'** the initial vowel is usually omitted, but in words beginning with **'em-'** the initial vowel is always written.

imagination	*immediate*	imitation	implement	imply

impression	improve	improvement	immigration

emphasis	empty	emerge	emergency	emigration

The '-us' ending

The S-circle is written to indicate the word ending **'-us'**;

generous	campus	numerous	famous	bonus

Where a double vowel sound is formed with the '-us' ending, as in **'-ious'**, it is indicated, as pronounced, by E + S; where necessary this may be disjoined. I + S may be written where it is more convenient, particularly after V).

Contemporary Shorthand

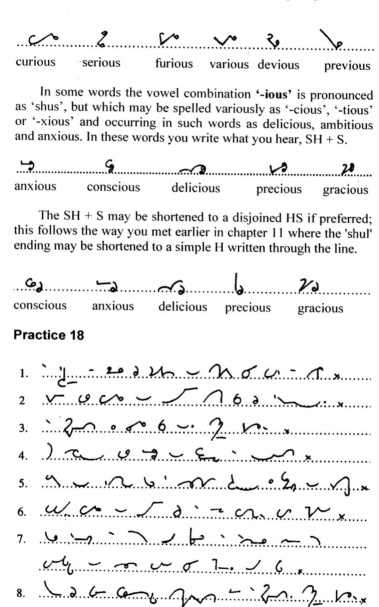

curious serious furious various devious previous

In some words the vowel combination '**-ious**' is pronounced as 'shus', but which may be spelled variously as '-cious', '-tious' or '-xious' and occurring in such words as delicious, ambitious and anxious. In these words you write what you hear, SH + S.

anxious conscious delicious precious gracious

The SH + S may be shortened to a disjoined HS if preferred; this follows the way you met earlier in chapter 11 where the 'shul' ending may be shortened to a simple H written through the line.

conscious anxious delicious precious gracious

Practice 18

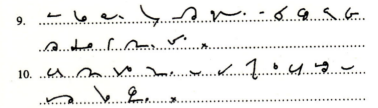

1. The application of science has helped to improve our way of life.
2. Everyone was curious to learn more about his adventures.
3. The government is serious about its immigration policy.
4. Her doctor was anxious to continue the treatment.
5. You-have to admit that a dismal picture is beginning to emerge.
6. We were curious to learn how the new committee would operate.
7. This evening the *chairman* will present the evidence on which we will be able to decide what our options will be.
8. There has been considerable improvement in the government's immigration policy.
9. In this city there are numerous supporters of our cause who have been most generous for many years.
10. We have made various *changes* to your report as we are anxious to address previous concerns

The End of the Beginning

You have now completed your study of Basic mode shorthand. You will have realized how simple and logical the system is and that you can customize it to suit your own way of writing.

But this is not the end of your potential for writing quick notes, it is only the end of the beginning. If you are writing notes several times a week, you will want to proceed to acquire some advanced techniques; these will increase your writing speed even further.

Contemporary Shorthand

The opportunity is there for you to write at speeds in excess of 100 words a minute. However, you need to be aware that writing at high speed is not merely a matter of learning the rules. The skill of high speed writing is one of listening to the spoken word and carrying it in your memory while writing the previous sentence. This skill comes with practice but this system of shorthand provides you with the necessary tools to achieve success.

In the following chapters will learn more about word abbreviation and further prefixes and suffixes. Using these features will add more fun and achievement to your note-taking.

How far you go is entirely in your hands but will be influenced by the frequency of your note-taking. The more often you write notes using shorthand the more familiar you will become with the system and the more skilled you will be in the use of this powerful system of fast writing.

Roy B. Tabor

16: Abbreviating principles

Abbreviating words

The primary objective in all shorthand writing is to abbreviate, and to reduce the time needed to record the words you hear. To this end you have seen how your normal handwriting can be streamlined into the simplified letters consisting of single pen strokes. This is a form of letter abbreviation. You have also seen how to write single letters or strokes to represent a number of word beginnings and word endings. In this chapter you are introduced to the essential principles of how to reduce long words to the shortest outline so that they can be easily recognized.

The context of a sentence is of considerable help to you in reading back what you have written. This allows you to leave out most short vowels and many lightly sounded consonants. Usually the longer the word the easier it is to abbreviate. You will find, therefore, that with long words it is not always necessary to write the whole word outline in full. You probably do this already when writing longhand notes. Many people will abbreviate such words as *'particular'* to partic., *'immediately'* to immed., and *'attention'* to attn.. We can apply this practice as a general principle;

☑ *Many long words can be clearly indicated by writing to the end of, or the consonant immediately following, the stressed syllable of the word.*

education   enthusiasm   certificate   impossible

The following examples illustrate this principle. Remember, however, that it is better to write the whole outline rather than to rely on a hastily devised abbreviation which is new to you. Often you can include a standard word ending for additional clarity. The more you write shorthand notes the more familiar you will become with the system and the easier it becomes to write and read the less familiar words.

Contemporary Shorthand

approximately	equivalent	attitude	individual

photograph	unanimous	particular	remarkable

opportunity	necessary	correspondence	especially

gentleman	important	memorandum	memoranda

The context of the sentence will usually make the meaning of each word clear. Thus, words which are formed from a common root may often be indicated sufficiently by writing only the root word. You will also find that the final syllable of a past tense verb may be omitted as its meaning will be clear from the context.

Thus ⌣ may represent *'satisfy', 'satisfaction',* or *'satisfactorily'.*

confer, conference, conferring	urgent, urgency, urgently

differ, difference, different	suggest, suggested, suggestion

origin, original, originality	administer, administration,

65

Roy B. Tabor

The plural of an abbreviated word is indicated in the normal way, by writing the S-dot.

universities   situations   attitudes   suggestions particulars

Practice 19

1.

2.

3.

4.

5.

6.

7.

8.

9.

10.

1. We must urgently ask you to attend to this problem immediately.
2. I think that this is now an entirely different ball-game.
3. The chairman is at present in conference so we suggest that you telephone later.

Contemporary Shorthand

4. This business is unlikely to-be completed immediately.
5. It-is always useful to adopt a positive attitude to life and people.
6. In this particular case we-are prepared to agree with your suggestion and will make the necessary changes in the proposal.
7. Please bring all your certificates when you attend for the meeting.
8. A good education is an excellent and necessary start to life.
9. May we take this opportunity to-thank-you for your enthusiastic help which you-have given in this matter..
10. 10.The recent Board meeting reached a unanimous decision regarding the merger of-the two *companies*.

17: Writing TR

The R position

In chapter 7 you were shown how to indicate PR by writing a normal length P above the line starting where a double-length P would begin. This is the R-position.

This principle is also applied to prefixes when they are used as separate words, especially **'extra-', 'over-'** and **'under-'**.

✓ *The sound of R is read after these prefixes written in the* *R-position.*

extra time	extra value	extra work	overcome	overlook

overtake	over dose	understand	understood	undertaken

The 'TR' principle

The R-position is used to indicate the sound of 'TR'; this occurs very frequently and you will find plenty of opportunities to use this powerful abbreviating device. You have already been introduced to a number of helpful prefixes, such as 'in-', 'en-', 'con-', and 'ex-'. The sound of 'TR' can be simply added to these prefixes to form 'intr-', 'entr-', 'contr-' and 'extr-'.

☑ *TR is read after any prefix which is disjoined and* *written in the R-position, preceding and above the outline.*

interest	contract	central	destroy	extreme

interfere	introduce	instruct	instruction	instrument

Contemporary Shorthand

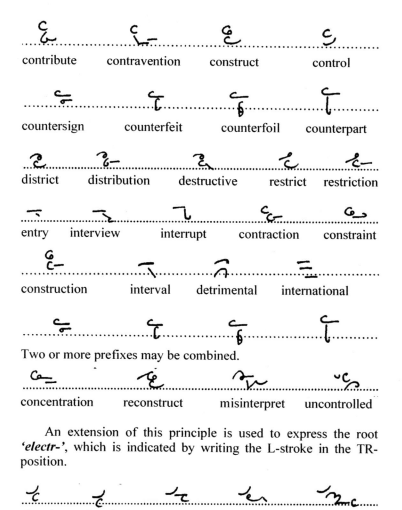

Two or more prefixes may be combined.

concentration   reconstruct   misinterpret   uncontrolled

An extension of this principle is used to express the root *'electr-'*, which is indicated by writing the L-stroke in the TR-position.

electric   electrical   electronic   electricity   electromagnetic

The 'TR' principle is not confined to the regular prefixes.

☑ *The sound of TR is read after any letter which is written in the R-position above the rest of the word outline.*

Roy B. Tabor

attract	distress	metropolitan	metric	detract

registered	contraction	illustrate	internal	external

astronomy	determine	veteran	attribute	industry

Practice 20

1.

2

3.

4.

5.

6.

7.

8.

9.

10.

1. It is in your best interests to follow their instructions carefully.
2. Although I-do-not control the contract I-am interested in the construction.
3. There-was a failure at the central electricity station.

4. I understand that-the alteration will mean much extra work.
5. Your contribution to-the interview was most appreciated.
6. We really cannot overlook the destructive nature of that man.
7. A new bridge is now under-construction across the river.
8. We do-not wish to interfere or place restrictions on your work.
9. Professional instruction is essential for an under-water diver.
10. Her latest history book is well illustrated in full color.

Writing 'TOR' and 'TURE'

Note, however, that where there is an intervening O or U vowel between the T and the R in the middle or at the end of a word, a double length T is written. This avoids any confusion with similar outlines using the TR principle.

restoration / restrain   extortion / external   contortion / contrition

lecture   picture   fracture   ligature   restore   storage

TR in phrases

The TR principle can be useful in writing some phrases.
✓ *'better'* is indicated by writing B in the TR position

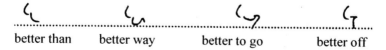

better than   better way   better to go   better off

Roy B. Tabor

Writing STR

The TR principle can be neatly and logically applied to represent the combination STR when it occurs at the beginning of a word by writing an S-dot above the outline.

✓ TR is read after the S-dot when it is written above the outline.

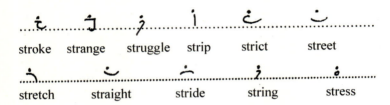

Practice 21

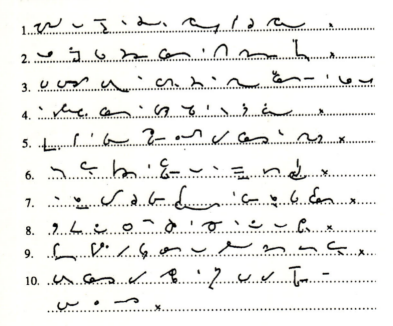

Contemporary Shorthand

1. I-would-like to interview the history lecturer after his lecture.
2. It-is strange that he-did-not consider a more modern approach.
3. We wondered whether the committee had the matter under-consideration at this time.
4. The architects considered the building to-be a very strong structure.
5. Plans for a better distribution system were considered at-the meeting.
6. Each country promised a contribution to the international aid project.
7. The external wall has been fractured and cannot easily be fixed.
8. She ran straight out of-the house and down the street to safety.
9. Federal forces are being used to restore order in-the country.
10. We-have considered your request and agree with your interpretation of what is needed.

Roy B. Tabor

18: Useful prefixes

Additional word beginnings

By now you will have realized how useful prefixes and suffixes can be in saving you time and by indicating words accurately. The following word beginnings do not occur quite so often as the ones you have met earlier; nevertheless you will meet them often enough to make them worth learning.

'anti-' *is expressed by a disjoined A + N.*

antibiotic	anti-social	anti-abortion	anti-freeze

'ante-' *may be expressed specifically by a disjoined A + NT.*

ante-natal	antecedent	ante-dated	ante-room

'circum-' *is expressed as a disjoined SR.*

circumference	circumspect	circumvent	circumnavigate

But note how the Quick Form **'circumstance'** and its derivatives are written;

circumstance	circumstances	circumstantial

'grand-' *is expressed by writing GRN,* because the final D is only lightly sounded it is omitted.

grandson	granddaughter	grandmother	grandstand

Contemporary Shorthand

'multi-' *is expressed as a disjoined M written through the line.*

multi-lateral   multi-purpose   multi-storey

'or-' *is indicated by a disjoined O indicator written as a superscript when it is followed by a consonant.*

orbit   order   organ   organization   but *ordinary*

'poly-' *is expressed as a disjoined P written through the line.*

polyester   polygamy   polygon   polymer   polyunsaturated

'semi-' *in compound words is written as a disjoined SM*

semi-final   semi-darkness   semi-detached   semi-circle

'sub-' *is indicated by writing an S-dot on the line.*

subtract   subdue   subject   submarine   submit

'super-' *is indicated by writing SU above the first letter of the outline.*

super, superintendent   superintend   supermarket   superficial

'trans-' *is indicated by TRS*

transaction   transfer   translation   transmit   transport

75

Roy B. Tabor

Practice 22

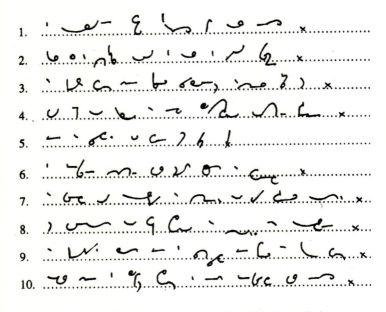

1. A translation can-be provided if it is needed.
2. This is a multipurpose tool and it-is a real bargain.
3. The police could only present circumstantial evidence against him.
4. We hope to visit the new supermarket tomorrow afternoon.
5. In the circumstances you cannot go wrong!
6. An anti-abortion demonstration was held outside the clinic.
7. The bank will transfer the money to your account to-day.
8. He wanted to keep secret the details of-the transaction.
9. The players stood in a semi-circle in front of their coach.
10. It-was only a superficial scratch and no anti-biotic was needed.

Contemporary Shorthand

19: Useful suffixes

More word endings

Here is a final group of word endings which will help you to write short and accurate outlines. They are all straightforward and easy to remember.

'-self' *is indicated by a disjoined SF written through the line.*

itself	herself	himself	myself	yourself	selfish

It is logical therefore, to indicate **'-selves'** by adding an S-dot to this ending.

'-ology' *is indicated by a disjoined J.*

'-ologist' *by J + S.*

'-ological' *by J + C written through the line.*

apology	meteorology	biology	psychology

geologist	zoologist	biologist	pathologist

biological	pathological	psychological

The alternative form for the prefix **'bio-'** may be preferred.

biology	biologist	biological	biography	biographical

77

Roy B. Tabor

'-graph' *is indicated by a disjoined G.*

'-graphy' *by G + E.*

'-graphic' *by GC*

'-graphical' *by GC written through the line*

'-gram' *is indicated by GR.*

telegraph	lithograph	autograph	calligraphy

geographic	biographical	geographical	telegram

'-hood' *is indicated by writing a disjoined H above the line.*

fatherhood	motherhood	falsehood	childhood	sainthood

'-ification' *is indicated by writing a disjoined F.*

classification	specification	modification	notification

'-lity' *is indicated by a disjoined subscript L.*

morality	quality	formality	finality	senility

reality	banality	actuality	sensuality	congeniality

'-ship' *is expressed as a disjoined SH.*

membership	worship	transship	authorship

Contemporary Shorthand

'-tic' *is indicated by a disjoined C on the line,* and
'-tical' *by writing a C disjoined through the line.*

| artistic | domestic | drastic | elastic | didactic | tactic |

| practical | fanatical | article | statistical | mystical |

'-ward' *is indicated by writing a disjoined W.*

| upward | awkward | downward | forward | inward | outward |

Practice 23

1.

2.

3.

4.

5.

Roy B. Tabor

1. The pathologist made a full autopsy report on the drowned man.
2. She is an outstanding student and has gained honours in both sociology and psychology.
3. The minister was asked to officiate at the ceremony.
4. Photography is my hobby and I look forward to photographing your anniversary celebrations and providing you with large color prints.
5. We-would-like to congratulate you on your success at-the university.
6. A degree in biology is a good start for a career in ornithology.
7. When you-have tabulated the results we can proceed to publication of-the experiment.
8. The value of your investments may appreciate but equally they may depreciate over time.
9. I-do-not-wish to speculate about her domestic situation.
10. I-will- not- be able to attend the next meeting; please will you make my apologies.

Contemporary Shorthand

20: All about numbers

Writing numbers

Numbers occur all the time; they are extremely important and must be written accurately at all times. Writing at speed can easily distort figures so it will pay you to study the following suggestions and practise writing them clearly without mistakes. Single figures should be reduced to their simplest form and the following are suggested as being economical and quick to write. Some writers like to make a circle around all numbers for extra clarity.

These numbers may be written in shorthand form if preferred.

Tens may be indicated by writing the E-indicator alongside the number.

Hundreds may be indicated by writing N beside the figure. (The N is a shortened form for *'hundred'*, otherwise written as HN)

81

Roy B. Tabor

✒ **Thousands may be indicated by writing N beneath the figure.** Alternatively the Quick form for 'thousand' (THO) may also be used.

2	5	6	9
2,000	5,000	6,000	9,000

✒ **Millions are indicated by writing M through the line next to the figure.**

2,000,000

Ordinals
To indicate the ordinals, *first, second, third,* **T is written beneath the figure.** This is used consistently for all numbers.

1	2	3	4	5	6	10
first	second	third	fourth	fifth	sixth	tenth

To make the adverbial form, just add the -LY suffix.

1	2	3	4
firstly	secondly	thirdly	fourthly

The letter forms may be used if preferred.

first	second	third	fourth

Contemporary Shorthand

Practice 24

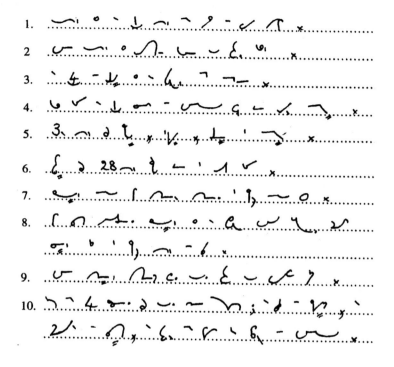

1. Today is the first day of the rest of your life.
2. When today is tomorrow then it becomes yesterday.
3. The Fourth of July is the birthday of-a nation.
4. This year the first snow of winter came in early November.
5. Thirty days has September, April, June and November.
6. February has twenty-eight days except in a leap year.
7. Saturday night for many means a special night out.
8. For some religions Saturday is the Sabbath while others hold Sunday as a special day of rest.
9. When Monday morning comes it's back to work again.

83

Roy B. Tabor

> 10. Each of the four seasons has its own charm; the joy of Spring, the glory of Summer, the beauty of the Fall and the festival of Winter.

Time

The time of day may be indicated as follows.

3 ⊂ *9 ∩* *5 ∩*

three o'clock   9 a.m.   5 p.m.

Years; When writing the *present century* you can omit the first two figures and write the N closely followed by the last two figures of the year. For other centuries the complete figures should be written in full.

−01   *1995*   *1865*   *1796*   *1620*

2001   1995   1865   1796   1620

The terms 'nineteenth century', 'eighteenth century' etc. may be expressed by writing SN following the year number. (Alternatively a common academic device is to enclose the year number within a large letter C).

19⌐ (19   *18⌐ (18*

nineteenth century   eighteenth century

Fractions

✎ Fractions are written as one figure above the other but without the usual intervening line.

The three most frequently occurring fractions can be quickly indicated by using an H for 'half', a crossed H for a 'quarter' and TH for 'three-quarters'.

4 ⟩   *2 ⊁*   *31 ⟍*

4 ½   2 ¼   31 3/4

Practice 25

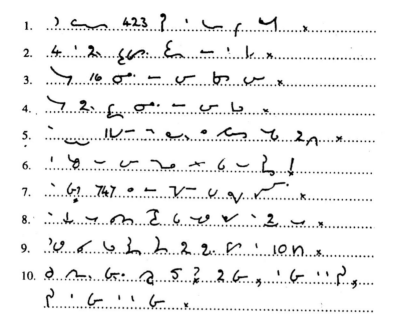

1. He counted 423 sheep and then fell asleep.
2. Four and twenty blackbirds baked in a pie.
3. There are sixteen ounces in one pound weight.
4. There are twenty fluid ounces in one pint.
5. The total population of the city is reckoned to be two million.
6. A thousand to one chance - but it happened!
7. The Boeing 747 is in operation with several airlines.
8. The first time seemed difficult but it was easier the second time.
9. He was sure that he had heard two shots fired at 10 p.m.
10. How many beans make five? Two beans, a bean and a half, half a bean and a bean.

Roy B. Tabor

Part Three
Alpha script level

Contemporary Shorthand

21: Writing Alpha level

This versatile method of shorthand can be written at two levels to meet the needs of both the professional and the general user of shorthand. Here in Part Three we show you how it can be written as an 'alphabetic' system.

Alpha-script level is for the occasional note-taker where very high writing speeds are not required. At this level you use your own familiar longhand letters instead of the simplified forms used in Basic mode.

☑ *The fundamental rules apply throughout the system.*

You will need to refer to Part One, Fundamental principles, before you proceed with the following chapters. The vowel indicator system is common throughout both levels.

The consonants

☑ *Consonants are written in their familiar longhand form, except T, D and N which are always written in their simplified forms.*

At Alpha level you use the familiar letters of your own handwriting. However it is recommended that you write letters without flourishes or unnecessary joining strokes. Try out the letters you will be using on a separate sheet of paper. When you are satisfied that you have found the most appropriate letter forms to use, write them in the following personal check-list as a reminder.

b	c	f	g	h	j	l

m	p	v	w	x	y	z

87

Roy B. Tabor

There is no mandatory right or wrong way to write a word outline; it can be tailored to individual requirements. The emphasis is on each person writing what is familiar; this aids initial learning, makes remembering easy and results in easily read outlines. The particular advantage of this shorthand method lies in its simple but powerful rules of abbreviation together with the use of the 'core letters'.

The sound of consonants

Words are written according to the way they sound. The following notes include comments on those consonants which have hard and soft forms.

The letter 'c' is used for the hard 'k' sound which occurs in the words, *cup, cat, act, luck, back* and *kick.*

K is only used to indicate '-*alk*' and for writing initials.

Note that the sound of 'f' may occur in different spellings as in the words, *fun, cliff, cough* and *photograph.*

The letter 'g' is used for the hard sound which occurs in the words, *go, gun, game, pig, log* and *dig.*

The letter 'j' is used for the soft 'g' sound which occurs in the words, *gin, jam, badge, dodge, wedge, jacket, gem* and *adjourn.*

The core letters

The core letters are a key feature of the method. They are the most frequently occurring consonants and receive special attention. At Alpha-script level, in order to gain the maximum writing speed with a minimum of new learning, three simplified letters of Basic mode are used.

☑ *D, T and N are written as simplified forms of the longhand letters.*

| D | T | N |

Contemporary Shorthand

D - this simple curve is the initial stroke of the longhand letter *d*.

T - this is the final stroke of the longhand letter *t*.

You may like to think of these signs as T, the lighter sound, which rises upwards, while D, the heavier sound, drops downwards.

(Ways of writing D and T are explored further in chapter 22).

N - straight as a Nail from eNd - to - eNd.

Writing vowels

✓ *The vowel indicators are used throughout the system.*

See Part One, Fundamental principles, for ways to indicate vowels.

The general rule is that *short vowels may be omitted in connected matter* where the context of the sentence guides you to the correct vowel. In the examples given throughout this text the vowel indicators are often included as these are stand-alone words. As familiarity increases you will soon discover that the short vowel indicators can easily be omitted when writing sentences.

The vowel indicators are used for final vowels and initial short vowels.

Significant long vowels can be written as necessary.

Normal longhand vowel letters may be used at Alpha level, if preferred

tune	new	buy	pay	tea	tie	know

gay	say	see, sea	sue	day	die

✎ An alternative fast and simple way to indicate a *long* vowel which occurs *in the middle of a word* is to write the relevant vowel indicator joined on to the final letter of the word outline. Refer back to Chapter 4 for the fast ways to indicate vowels.

89

Roy B. Tabor

p̢ *(pa_)*　　**s̢** *(si_)*　　**fç** *(fac)*　　**b̢** *(bo_)*
pain　　　　　sign　　　　　fake　　　　　bone

Writing the word outline

Now that you have been introduced to the consonants and the vowel system you can begin to write more words.

gv̄　　**b̄c**　　**lg**　　**mp**　　**ms**　　**w̄**　　**ḡ**
given　　bank　　leg　　map　　miss　　win　　gun

It is important that each letter is formed clearly; don't scribble your letters as this will only lead to confusion. Get into the habit of writing precise letters at this stage and you will soon be able to write faster with practice. Remember that the word outline is a skeleton of essential consonants with any significant vowels added for clarity.

Practice A 1

Write out the following examples several times. Remember, the more practice you have in writing shorthand the more fluent you will become.

čb, bo̅, g̊p, fç, l̢₇, p̲, p̲,
p̲c, p̲, p̲, p̲c, p̲, pes, p̲c̲c,
pip, va_, v̄, v̄, v̄v, v̲ , svc .

cab, bone, gap, fake, line, pin, pen,
pink, pain, pan, panic, pay, peace/ piece, picnic,
pipe, vein / vain, vine, van, venue, view, civic.

Quick forms

There are a number of commonly occurring words which are given special Quick Forms, much as you abbreviate such words as – *road* rd, *amount* amt, and *avenue* ave, in normal writing. They are given special attention simply because they occur so

Contemporary Shorthand

frequently. You probably use some of these abbreviated words already when you write notes.

These most commonly occurring words are presented in two groups, in order of their frequency. Together these few words form about a quarter of all spoken and written language.

Group 1 Quick Forms

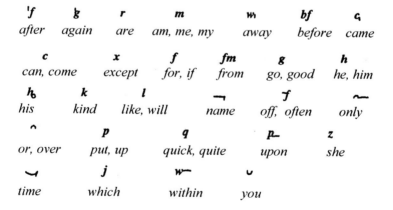

The next group of words is equally important, as altogether the two groups make up almost half of all written matter. By learning and using these words you will be able to write some fifty per cent of every thing you will ever need.

Group 2 Quick Forms

'f	ğ	r	m	wı	bf	ꞓ
after	again	are	am, me, my	away	before	came

c	x	f	fm	g	h
can, come	except	for, if	from	go, good	he, him

h₆	k	l	⇁	ꞙ	～
his	kind	like, will	name	off, often	only

⌒	p	q	p―	z
or, over	put, up	quick, quite	upon	she

⌣	j	w―	ᴗ
time	which	within	you

Roy B. Tabor

Practice A 2

1. *c h w⁓ ` gam ⸺ ⸺ ?*
2. *⌣ s v g ⁻ ⌣ ⌣ c w m ˎ*
3. *` m⁻ h⁀ ' v b⁀ cf ˎ*
4. *w⁓ s ` ⊣ ⁻` m⸺ w ` g⸺ ?*
5. *j wˏ ⤳ h g ʄ ` gam ws ^ ?*

    1.   Can he win the game in time?
    2.   It is very good of you to come with me.
    3.   The man had a very bad cough.
    4.   What is the name of the man with the gun?
    5.   Which way did he go after the game was over?

Contemporary Shorthand

22: Writing T and D

Writing T and D

The letters T and D are particularly important as so often they form part of the past tense of verbs. You will find that they occur in every sentence so you will get plenty of practice in writing them. At Alpha-level we use only the *simplified forms of these longhand letters*; both are derived from their longhand equivalents. Remember that T, the lighter sound, curves upward, while D, the heavier sound, curves downward.

| wet | sat | bed | fed | mad | had | led |

✓ *When T follows N, it may be modified to a small hook; this is always written anti-clockwise.*

| bent | want | sent | went |

✓ *Similarly, D is written as a clockwise hook following N;*

| bend | send | find | end | hand | lend | mend |

The T and D hooks are also used after T and D respectively;

stet   did

When the sounds of T and D follow each other they are written as a continuous double curve.

| wanted | scented | rotted | wetted | debt | hunted |

Roy B. Tabor

✐ When T follows C the latter may be extended in a single curve.

act	tact	sect	defect	*but* acted

Practice A 3

1. *m ᴗ s ↝ ` p̀ bc ᴗ ᴗ* ✗
2. *ᴗ ws g ˉᴗ ᴗ L, m ` p̀* ✗
3. *ᴧ ᴝ wᵌ ᴗ ᴗ s, h wᵢ* ✗
4. *h wᴗ ᴗ p ` m. ᴗ ` bc* ✗
5. *h ᴗc ` wp fm ` ᴧ m* ✗

   1. I meant to send the pen back to you.
   2. It was good of you to lend me the pen.
   3. I do not want you to send him away.
   4. He wanted to put the money in the bank.
   5. He took the weapon from the dead man.

Writing TH

The combination double consonant TH is represented by a simplified T slanted downwards.

✓ *TH is indicated by writing T at a downward slope.*
The TH-stroke represents the words, *than, thank* and *thing*.

that	they	them	thick, think	then	though

both	method	path	death	thief	thigh

Here are some useful combination words with '**thing**'.

nothing	anything	everything	something

94

Contemporary Shorthand

Practice A 4

1. *w v g⌣ ⌣ fɔ ' ⌣ m⌣ ⌣ bɔ ` pip*
2. *ʋ h ⌢ ws mɔ ⌣ mꞔ h wl⌣*
3. *' ⌣ ⌣ h ws ⌐ ' ⌣ ⁻ pa⌐*
4. *z s⌢ ⌣ h w⌐ ⌐o ʋ ⌐ ⌐*
5. *⌐ ⌣ c fɔ ` ʀ⌐ ⌣ fl⌐*

 1. We have got to find a new method to bend the pipe.
 2. Everything he did was meant to make him wealthy.
 3. I think that he was in a lot of pain.
 4. She said that he would know everything in time.
 5. Only you can find the path to follow.

Writing final '-te' and '-de' (Syllable T and D)

✓ *A vowel indicator written in the superscript position, indicates the relevant long vowel followed by T or D.*

f`	*g'*	*l´*	*b⁻*	*c˘*	*w'*
feet	gate	light	boat	cute	wait, weight

f'	*⌐*	*w´*	*l⁻*	*f⌐*	*m'*
fade	deed	wide	load	food	made

It is rarely necessary to distinguish between T and D. However, a T is always read as a default; a D may be added to the vowel indicator for a positive indication.

Notice that a *final long vowel* is always written on the line beside the final consonant, whereas the - *'te* and - *'de* vowel indicators are written clearly above the line. Compare the following;

f.	*f`*	*⌣,*	*⌣´*	*w₁*	*w'*	*g,*	*g´*
fee	feet	tie	tight	way	wait	guy	guide

95

Roy B. Tabor

A final '**-ed**' is indicated by adding D to the vowel indicator and a plural S-dot may be used as appropriate.

stated	heated	guided	writes	gates

If a 'positive' D has been written a D-hook may be added for the final '-ed' syllable.

To indicate the ending '**-uate**', the U sign is written before the final '-ate'.

insinuate	actuate	evaluate	punctuate

Practice A 5

1. *w⁓ ⌣ g⌣ l' h m' hs w, ⌣ ` b⁻ ×*
2. *f ∪ c f⌐ ` r' r⁻ bc w l⁻ b l' ×*
3. *` c⁻ h f⌐ ⌐ ` l' -` ċ ×*
4. *v ⌐, m' ` ⌐ r⁻ ● w' ● w ⌐ ?*
5. *z m' ` g l, b⁻ s' -` g' ×*

     1.   When it got light he made his way to the boat.
     2.   If you can find the right road back we will not be late.
     3.   The coat had faded in the light of the sun.
     4.   Have they made the new road as wide as we need?
     5.   She made the dog lie by the side of the gate.

Contemporary Shorthand

23: The sound of R

Consonant R

☑ *R is read after any consonant or core letter which is doubled in size.*

This means that longhand letters are written as capitals and the simplified letters (D, T and N) are doubled in length.

CR *C* ,   FR *F* ,   GR *G* ,   PR *P* ,   DR ⌐ ,   TR ⌣

C,	*F*	*C𝑣*	*G'*	*Gb*	*C'*
cry	free	crew	grade	grab	crate

G𝗂	*F'*	*F⌐*	*G⌐*	*P𝗂*	*P'*
gray	freight	friend	grand	pray	pride

⌐c	⌐g	⌣	⌣	⌣
drink	drug	try	truth	trade

Syllable R

Following the principle that short and unstressed vowels are generally omitted, a double-size letter may be used where there is an intervening short vowel (syllable R). Where necessary the relevant short vowel indicator may be written above the word outline. In practice you will find it rarely necessary to insert a short vowel indicator when the words occur in connected matter; the context of the sentence will almost always indicate the precise meaning of the word.

C⌐	*C⌐*	*R*	*F*	⌣	⌐c	*Pc*	*C*
card	court	part	far	turn	dark	park	car

⌐	⌐	w⌐	⌐	⌐	⌐	r⌐
either	neither	weather	north	other	another	rather

sM	*Mc*	*rC⌐*	*W*	*S⌣*	*U*
summer	American	record	were	sort	your

Roy B. Tabor

Fs	*Ws*	*Cs*	𝒞	⌒	W⁻
force	worse	course	court	dirt	warn
⌐ᐯ	*Sv*	*bG*	b⌣	∟⌣	*rMc*
never	serve	bigger	better	letter	remark

✍ When a *long vowel* occurs between the consonant and the R, the relevant lower case vowel letter is normally written. This is faster to write than a capital letter vowel which would also be permissible.

ca	*pu*	*–e*	*fi*	⌒*a*	*e*	*wa*
care	pure	near	fire	dare	*here*	where

sca	*fe₀*	*fa*	*ba*	· *re*	⌒*e*
scare	fierce	fair	bear	rear	dear

The same principle is applied when R follows an initial vowel.

a⌣	*agᵥ*	*av*	*ec⌣*	*i⌐*	*uj*
art	argue	arrive	erect	iron	urge

ub⁻	*uj⌐*	*e⌣*	*e⌐*→	*og⁻*	*ob⌣*
urban	urgent	earth	earned	organ	orbit

But note that when a D or T is followed by a long vowel I + R, a double-length consonant is written with an added I-vowel indicator.

⌣✓	r⌣✓	⌐⌣
tire	retire	dire

✍ An upper case, or capital, letter is used to indicate a final *–er* in these words;

nearer ⌐*E*   dearer ⌐*E*   rarer *rA*

Contemporary Shorthand

A separate R may be used to represent the prefix *'para-' pr*;

prs'   **pr⌒P**   **prm⌒c**

parasite   paratrooper   paraffin

Note the following use of TR or DR after a long vowel; a normal vowel letter makes an easier join with a following TR, but a vowel indicator makes an easy join with DR.

wa   **be**   **ca**   **r**   **l**   **w**

waiter   beater   cater   raider   leader   wider

The Quick Form *'for'* is *f*; this is used for words beginning with the word 'for'.

fgv   **fg**   **fW**   **fg**   **fg**

forgive   forget   forward   forgotten   forgo

Note that there is a Quick Form for *'ever'* and *'every'* *V*, which is used in the following combinations;

V   **Vb**   **V**   **Vw**

everyone   everybody   every time   every way

Practice A 6

1. *h w r P w hs wf gv w hs C*

2. *he c w B pu a b hl*

3. *z Pc C F CPc*

4. *FM h W fi B m' B l*

5. *ws c g s mc cmp*

    1.   He would rather part with his wife than give away his car.

    2.   Only here can we breathe pure air and be healthy.

    3.   She tried to park the car at the far end of the car-park.

Roy B. Tabor

4. The farmer had warned that the fire in the barn might burn all night.
5. It was too dark to go on so they decided to make camp.

Writing 'than'

'Comparison' words such as 'better', 'wetter', and 'bigger' are usually followed by 'than'; these phrases are easily written.

E	*E*	*M*	*a*
nearer than	dearer than	more than	quicker than

Word endings '-ly' and '-ty'

The word ending *'-ly'* is indicated by writing the E-vowel at the end of the outline and *just below the line.*

q,	*m*	*ra,*	*k*	*ls,*	*l,*
quickly	mainly	rarely	*kindly*	lastly	*likely*

The word ending '*-ty*' may be indicated by writing the E-indicator *on the line.*

cv	*pV,*		*cps,*	*sca,*
cavity	poverty	identity	capacity	scarcity

After the word ending '-te' the '-ly' indicator may be written directly below the preceding E-vowel. This obviates the jump that would otherwise be needed to write the '-ly' below the line. The following examples demonstrate how this works;

l	*s*	*_*	*sC*	*_*	*rm*
lately	sedately	neatly	discreetly	tightly	remotely

Contemporary Shorthand

Practice A 7

1. ` *C* ws *M* *h* ᴄ 'F⌐ ₓ
2. *w⌐* ˅ *PF* ᵕ *m* ' *8* *r* ᴗ *7* ?
3. *w* *H⌐* ᴗ ` *C* ws *b* — ⁼˙ *rpa* ₓ
4. *z* ᴗ ᵕ *Pc* *H* *C* *E* ᵕ ` *g* ⁻ ` *Mc* ₓ
5. ` *mɹ* *sm* ᵕ *lv* — ~ᵢ *pV* ₓ

1. The car was more than he could afford.
2. Would you prefer to meet at eight rather than seven?
3. We heard that the car was badly in need of repair.
4. She tried to park her car nearer to the gate of the market.
5. The majority seemed to live in dire poverty.

Roy B. Tabor

24: The sounds of S and Z

Writing S and Z

The sounds of S and Z are the most commonly occurring sounds in the English language. S occurs in every sentence and it is a principal indicator of plural words. Because it is so frequent it deserves special attention.

✓ *At the beginning of a word a normal letter S is written.*

sad, said	same	send	save	see	second

It may also be used in the middle, or at the end, of a word.

reserve	concern	escape	easy	pass

✓ *The simplified letter S, may be used in the middle of, or at the end of, a word.* This S-circle is derived from the upper part of the longhand letter. It provides an easy join between two letters. However, its use is *optional* and, where a high writing speed is not critical, a familiar S may be preferred.

design	vestige	lesson	missed	distance	course
as	business	visit	visitor	worse	missed

A letter S can be written to indicate a final '*-st*', omitting the 't'.

guest	test	best	west	cost	dust

Contemporary Shorthand

But after the '-te' indicator the S-circle is more easily written.

—ᵇ	lᵃ	lᵇ	sᵇ	⌣ᵃ	wᵃ
neatest	lightest	latest	sadist	tightest	widest

✓ *The sound of Z is indicated by a normal longhand Z.*

jz	*ze-*	*Caz*	*Fez*	*baz*	*lZ*
jazz	zero	craze	freeze	blaze	laser

Plural S

✐ To indicate a plural word ending in S, the S-circle is reduced to an S-dot. This is always used to indicate the plural of an abbreviated word.

g·	⌣•.	*l.*	*b⁻·*	*bc.*	⌢*sc.*	*rsc.*
goods	*times*	*likes*	boats	books	desks	risks

✐ Use the S-dot as convenient, to indicate a final 's' sound.

c.	*fⁿ*	⌢''	*b`·*	*ca*⌣•	*f*⌣•.
comes	fights	dates	beats	caters	fighters

Practice A 8

spᴄ, s̀p, sp̀⁀, s⌣c, s̈- , sm , s₁
s⸱ , s⁀ , s̀c , s̀⌣c , gs , ms , ws
Cs , ⸲s , ls , Ps , ⸲ , ⌣ₑ , ⸯ
⁀ₑ , 'vi̶ₑ , rvi̶ₑ , spaₑ , pleₑ

speak, step, spend, stick, sun, some, say,
see, send, sack, sink, guess, miss, was,
cross, use, less, press, this, these, nice,
niece, advise, revise, space, police

Roy B. Tabor

Double 'ses'

✓ The double 'ses' sound as in 'crisis' and 'sister', is indicated by writing a disjoined S (or an S-circle if preferred).

system	suspect	sister	assist	assisted	resisted
crisis	census	success	basis	insist

For words ending in S, the S-dot is used to indicate a *plural* 'ses' word; the S-circle followed by the plural S-dot is preferred.

senses	cases	pieces	races	fences	fuses

The prefixes 'con-' and 'com-'

There are many words beginning with these general prefixes; they may occur as **con-, com-, cam-** or **cum-**. All of these are represented by the letter 'c'.

content	continue	concert	consisted	consent
contain	container	compare	*computer*	comparison

(If preferred, 'com-' may be indicated positively by writing a disjoined 'c'.)

The prefixes **'can-'** and **'coun-'** are represented by writing 'C + N'.

candid	cancer	candy	count	counter	county

Contemporary Shorthand

Practice A 9

1. It was sad that he had to sell his business so quickly.
2. We must press for a new subway to cross such a wide road.
3. It is easy to miss your way unless you can read a map.
4. In some sense it could be said that she has second sight.
5. The sun sets in the west every night.

Roy B. Tabor

25: The L endings

Consonant L

The longhand letter L may be used at any time.

L	*lp*	*lo*	*cl*	*lf*	*l*	*lc*
line	lip	alone	collide	life	delete	luck

✓ *L may be omitted in the consonant combinations, BL, CL, FL, GL, PL, SL*

bc	*cc*	*fo*	*g*	*pa*	*l*
black	click	flown	glitter	plane	slot

Final syllable L

☑ *L may be omitted at the end of a word; the final L sound may be indicated positively by writing the previous letter through or below the line.*

caf	*sf*	*b*	*b*	*cp*	*fm*
careful	useful	double	trouble	couple	formal

Words of one syllable ending in L may be indicated by writing the initial letter through, or below, the line.

e.g. kill, fill, full, tell, hill, pill, sell.

Words incorporating the syllable 'al-' are indicated by '*l*';

l	*lms*	*l*	*lw*	*lr*	*l*
all	almost	although	*always*	*already*	alter
l	*fl*	*cl*	*bl*	*wl*	*sml*	*ml*
tall	fall	call	ball	wall	small	mall

Contemporary Shorthand

The word endings '**-ual**' and '**-ule**' are indicated by writing the U-indicator through or below the line.

m⌢ᵤ	⌢ᵤ	*cps*ᵤ	*G*—ᵤ ·	*mlc*ᵤ	⌒cᵤ
module	nodule	capsule	granule	molecule	ridicule

⌐ᵤ	⌐ᵤ,	*G*⌒	*G*⌒ᵤ.	⌒	*vs*ᵤ
actual	actually	gradual	gradually	dual	visual

The ending '**-ulate**' is indicated by writing U + A through or below the line.

*spc*ᵤ	*rg*ᵤ	*s*⌒*m*ᵤ	⌒*b*ᵤ	*ps*ᵤ
speculate	regulate	stimulate	tabulate	postulate

✎ Note how the following words may be written using this rule.

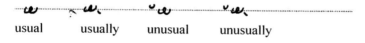

usual	usually	unusual	unusually

'-bility'

The word ending '**-bility**' is simply indicated by writing a disjoined
B + E through the line.

'*b*,	⌒*s*ᵦ.	*cp*ᵦ.	⌒.	*fs*ᵦ.
ability	disability	capability	inability	feasibility

*Pb*ᵦ.	*rsp*⌒*s*ᵦ.	⌒*b*.	*ps*ᵦ.
probability	responsibility	debility	possibility

Roy B. Tabor

Practice A 10

1. ⌐ *r* *m⌐c* *res⌐.* ' *h* *z⌐* *b* *caf* – ⌣ ⌢ ⌣ ×
2. ⌐*s* '*mp* ⌣ *bf* *w* →⌣ *lv* *f* ⌐ *aℛ* ×
3. ⌐*s* *V* *psb* ⌣ *h* *l* *bb* ⌣ *lv* ' —*m* *lf* ⌣
4. ⌣ *ws* *psb* ⌣ *s.* ⌐ *b⌐* ' *g* *m,* *f* *Z* ×
5. ⌣ *s* ' *Gv* *Po s* ' *ms* *b* ⌐ *caf.* *f* ⌣ *s* ⌣ *scs⌐* ×

   1. There are medical reasons why he should be careful not to do that.
   2. There is ample time before we need to leave for the airport.
   3. There is every possibility that he will be able to live a normal life.
   4. It was possible to see the boat a good mile off-shore.
   5. It is a gradual process and must be done carefully if it is to succeed.

Contemporary Shorthand

26: H and its combinations

Writing H

H is often very lightly sounded when it occurs at the beginning of a word and in such cases it can often be omitted. Note the Quick Form for 'who' and 'whom' where the vowel indicator is written on its side to distinguish it from 'you'.

		om	*op*	*i*
who, whom	whose	home	hope	higher

h	*h*	*h*	*h*	*hp*	*h*	*hb*
he, him	his, has	had	hand	happen	high	habit

✐ Note how the following frequent word groups are written.

h	*h s*	*h.*	*h s.*
has, his	he is	he's	he says

When R follows H, a capital letter H is used following the general rule for indicating the sound of R.

H	*H*	*H*	*Hm*	*H wa*
her	heard, hard	heart	harm	hardware

H	*H*	*H s*
hurry	horrid	harass

Double consonants CH, SH. Writing CH

✓ *CH is represented by the letter 'J'.*

Note the similarity of sound between soft 'j' and 'ch', e.g. badge, batch, where the 'd' is only lightly sounded.

j	*y*	*bj*	*rj*	*⌐j*	*sj*
which	each	batch	reach	teach	such

109

Roy B. Tabor

jc	j-	mj	rj	fj	jp	je.
check	chin	much	rich	fetch	chop	cheers

A following R sound is indicated by writing a capital letter *J*.

∨J	cJ		SJ	⌐	Jm	wJ
teacher	catcher		searcher	chart	charm	watcher

Writing SH

☑ *SH is represented by the letter 'z'.*

z	z⌐	zp	z-	z⌣	zc	cz
she	should	shop	show	shoe	shock	cash

fz	wz	f-z	rz	rz	ps⌐
fish	wish	finish	vanish	rush	pushed

R is added to SH in the usual way by writing a capital letter Z.

Z-c	Z⌐	Z-,	pZ	fZm	wZ
shrink	shred	shrine	pusher	fisherman	washer

The word **'sure',** and in combinations, is also represented by Z.

Z	'Z	mZ	sZ	lZ	PZ
sure	assure	measure	censure	leisure	pressure

Writing QU

☑ *The combination QU, usually pronounced as 'kw', is represented by the letter 'q'.*
(The distinctive simplified form is written as a crossed 'q' and may be preferred, see chapter 10.)

q	Q	q⌐	q⌐	qs
quick, quite	*quicker*	*quickly*	quit	*question*

Contemporary Shorthand

rqi	*⁻qi*	*Q*	*ɗqi*	*cC*	*lC*
require	inquire	inquiry	acquire *BUT* conquer		lacquer

Practice A 11

1. *r ʋ Z ∪ z ᴄ z wⁿ f⁻z Wc ' 9?*
2. *∟ c b − qs ᵇ ∪ ˋ rsl∪ −ˋ Q.* ˟
3. *H jf 'Z∖ H ∪ z wⁿ c ∪ − Hm* ˟
4. *w H⁻ ∪ z h∖ ∪ H. ∪ cj ˋ pa∟* ˟
5. *h wz∖ ∪ ʋ ˋ cz ⌐ h⌐ bf h wⁿ fnz ˋ jb* ˟

1. Are you sure that she said she would finish work at nine?
2. There can be no question as to the result of the inquiry.
3. Her chief assured her that she would come to no harm.
4. We heard that she had to hurry to catch the plane.
5. He wished to have the cash in hand before he would finish the job.

The 'shun' ending

The word ending pronounced '*shun*', occurs very frequently; it is spelled variously as '-tion', '-sion' and '-cian'. For many years it has been an accepted convention among writers and printers to shorten these endings to a small 'n' written at the end of the word above the line. This practice is also followed in Alpha-level.

✓ *The 'shun' word ending is indicated by writing a disjoined simplified* N.

⁻c⌐	*m⌐*	*⁻P⌐*	*ɗ⌐*	*˘Cp⌐*
direction	mention	operation	action	description

Keep this close to, but separate from, the last letter of the word and above the line. It is not usually necessary to insert the

Roy B. Tabor

preceding vowel indicator as the context will normally give the meaning of the word. However, where a stressed long vowel precedes the shun-ending the relevant vowel indicator may be included if preferred.

station	occasion	location	edition	quotation	nation

condition	reservation		corporation	suggestion

The plural of these words is indicated by writing a final S-dot.

actions	positions	sections	conditions	corporations

The shun-N is written *below the line* to indicate **'-tional'**.

directional	occasional	operational	national	rational

The shun -N is doubled in length in the usual way to indicate the addition of a following R sound.

practitioner	pensioner	petitioner	conditioner

The 'shunt' ending

✓ *The word ending pronounced 'shunt' and spelled as '-cient or '-tient' is indicated by the Shun-N + T-hook.*

'**-ciently**' is similarly indicated with the addition of -LY (the E-indicator written below the line), and

'**-ciency**' by Shun-N + SE.

efficient	deficient	sufficient	patient	impatient

efficiently	sufficiently	patiently	impatiently

Contemporary Shorthand

ʻf—ᴇ
efficiency

sf—ᴇ
sufficiency

ʻf-ᴇ
deficiency

The 'shul' ending

There is an associated word ending which is pronounced as *'shul'* and spelled usually as '-cial'. This is indicated by writing a disjoined 'z' (SH) through or below the line.

sp$_z$
special

P$_z$
partial

p—$_z$
potential

ʻf$_z$
official

cM$_z$
commercial

f—$_z$
financial

ᴢ—$_z$
essential

—$_z$
initial

a f$_z$
artificial

Cu$_z$
crucial

cf—$_z$
confidential

Practice A 12

1. w~ ꞓ— ᴧ ᴜ ꞟ ⤸z.   ?
2. ᴜ s ` ⸚ᴏ— z ꞓ ᴜ ⸚v ᴜ ` ᴤ⹁— ✗
3. h σ ꞡ ' ꞇ⸗ ⸚ꞓ — σ⁀ ᴜ b so$_z$ ˬ
4. ` ʻf$_z$ ᴤsCp— s ᴜ ᴧ ws ' sc s$_f$ ꞏPa— ✗
5. ᴜ ms b ᴃ ·r— ' pa⸚ ⹀ ᴤs ᴤᴜ— ✗

    1.   What action did you take initially?
    2.   That is the direction she took to drive to the station.
    3.   He only takes an occasional drink in order to be social.
    4.   The official description is that it was a successful operation.
    5.   You must be both rational and patient in this situation.

Roy B. Tabor

27: Diphthongs

Writing AW

The sound of AW has a number of different spellings and is pronounced variously in different parts of the country. It may occur as *'ought'*, *'bought'*, *'fought'*, and is essentially a variant of the vowel 'O'.

In normal speech this is also heard in such words as *haul, hall, fall* and *tall,* and again in *law, saw* and *awesome.* Because Alpha-level is written according to the sound of words, and allowing for geographical variants in pronunciation, we can use the same vowel for all these words.

☑ *The sound of AW is indicated by 'w'.*

(The simplified form is a narrow 'o', the O + U vowel indicators, see chapter 12.)

w~	bw~	fw~	cw~	~w~
ought	bought	fought	caught	taught

But the AW may be omitted in some common words.

~	w~	c~
daughter	water	caught

The prefix **'auto-'** can be logically indicated by writing AW disjoined.

w mbl	w C~	w mc	wm~
automobile	autocrat	automatic	automated

Writing '-alk'

'*k*' represents the combination **'-alk'**.

tk	wk	wk~	jk	bk
talk	walk	walked	chalk	balk

Contemporary Shorthand

Diphthongs 'ow' and 'oi'

These diphthongs are combinations of two vowel sounds pronounced as a single syllable. Each has its own distinctive indicator.

☑ *OW is indicated by the longhand letter 'o'.*

o	⌣σ	‑σ	ᴕ‑	ᴕ‑	*oV*	*foᴗ*
out, how	town	now	down	doubt	however	found
soᴗ	*lo*	*Boᴗ*	*smo*		*roᴗ*	*os*
sound	allow	brown	somehow		round	house
op	*oG‑*	*ol⌣*	*olᵥ*	*ol⌐*		
output	outgrow	outlet	outlay	outline		

The sound of R is added to OW by writing a capital letter '*O*'.

pO	*fO*	⌣O	*zOᴖ*
power	flower, flour	tower	showered

☑ *OI is indicated by 'y'*
(The alternative form is simplified AW + E, see chapter 10.)

jy‑	*cy‑*	*'vy‑*	*r,*	*vy*	⌣,	‑ys	*s,*
join	coin	avoid	royal	void	toil	noise	soil

Further word beginnings and endings

As you have seen, a single letter can usefully represent a whole initial or final syllable. The ones used in Alpha-level occur often and each one is associated with a related letter or sound and is easily remembered.

Because you will use these so frequently you will find that they become very familiar and reading them back is soon automatic. As with all skills regular practice and use are the keys to proficiency.

115

Roy B. Tabor

'en-, in-, un-'

For words beginning with 'en-' and 'in-' the initial vowel indicator is usually omitted. A U-indicator written on the line represents the prefix 'un-'.

These prefixes occur very often and so, literally at a stroke, you can add a significant number of words to your shorthand vocabulary.

enough	enter	inform	invade	instead	intend

unable	until	unlike	uncover	unless

Practice A 13

1. *H ᴛ⁓ ∀ ᵘₛ⤸ ⌣ s₁ 'ho ⤳ Bσ⁻ co'* ₓ
2. *h fσ⁀ H V O ⌁⸍ ` O* ₓ
3. *ᵘ ᴄ⌁ H꜉ 'vy⌁ mcg ᐧ ⁻ys ⌁ ↳ ℒᵤ⁻* ₓ
4. *` ⌁⸍ Cσ⁻ os′ ⁻ os zo⌁⸍ w jy* ₓ
5. *⌣ ws ᵛ⸑, b ⁻ ᵛ⁻σ⁻ , ⌣ g⸑ sj ᐧ fᵤ rsp⸌* ₓ

    1. Her diction teacher used to say 'How now brown cow'.

    2. He phoned her every hour on the hour.

    3. You could hardly avoid making a noise in that situation.

    4. The entire crowd outside the house shouted with joy.

    5. It was unusual, but not unknown, to get such an official response.

Contemporary Shorthand

Writing the '-ng' ending

This word ending occurs frequently as '-ing' and forms the present participle of verbs, eg. *writing, eating, drinking, sleeping.* It also occurs in such words as *long, sung, hang* and *belong.*

✓ *The ending '-ng' may be indicated by 'g'.*

seg	e-g	⌐-cg	ʅ-g	m-g	⌐ug
seeing	eating	drinking	sending	meeting	during

⌐g	og	L-g	⌐g	flog	Bog
thanking	owing	landing	sitting	following	borrowing

sg	hg	wg	rg	lg-	lg
song	hang	wing	wrong	length	lung

The sound of R is added to NG by writing a capital letter *G*.

fG	lG	sG	hG	hG	yG
finger	longer	singer	hunger	hungry	younger

✐ When the NG- ending is itself followed by '-ing' it is disjoined and written above the line in the superscript position.

h^s	s^s	bl^s	r^s	l^s	B^s
hanging	singing	belonging	ringing	longing	bringing

The L-rule is applied to this word ending in the usual way, by writing the '-ng' through or below the line.

$j_ɛ$	$s_ɛ$	$'_ɛ$	⌐$_ɛ$	$m_ɛ$
jungle	single	angle	triangle	mingle

At the beginning of a word the 'NG' is preceded by the relevant vowel indicator;

'G	'G⟍	'GL	ɣL⸱⸱	ɣlz⸱
anger	angry	angler	England	English

117

Roy B. Tabor

But note that NG is not used in those words where the hard or soft G is pronounced;

Ɡaj	꞊	꞊js	h꞊j	꞊j-e
engage	engine	ingest	hinge	engineer

✎ A fast alternative way to indicate the 'ng' ending is to use a simplified '*g*' written half-size (see chapter 13).

s꞉	h꞉	w꞉	B꞉	s꞉
song	hang	wing	bringing	singing

'-ment' and '-mount'

Both these word endings, **'-ment' and '-mount'** are represented by the letter '*m*'.

cm	꞊cm	꞊m	mom	꞊m	'm
comment	document	element	moment	treatment	amount

This suffix becomes '**-mental**' in the usual way of adding 'L' by writing the '*m*' through the line.

f꞊$_m$	꞊$_m$	꞊$_m$
fundamental	elemental	departmental

'-tive'

The word ending '**-tive**' is simply represented by the letter '*v*'.

cPv	cꞬv	mov	ꞔv	ꞙcv	rlv
comparative	competitive	motive	active	effective	relative

118

Contemporary Shorthand

Practice A 14

1. (shorthand outline)
2. (shorthand outline)
3. (shorthand outline)
4. (shorthand outline)
5. (shorthand outline)

1. They continued eating and drinking all night.
2. The singer needed treatment for her sore throat.
3. I am sure that this time the treatment will be effective.
4. For a moment I thought I was seeing double.
5. The following comments should be noted.

Roy B. Tabor

28: All about X

Writing X

✓ *The sound of X is indicated by the longhand letter 'x'.*

mx	*bx*	*fx*	*—x*	*wx*	*sx*
mix	box	fix	index	wax	sex

✎ Where appropriate the previous letter may be crossed to form the letter 'x'.

next	tax	text

Writing 'ex-'

✓ The prefix **'ex-'** occurs frequently; *it is expressed by 'x'.*

xc	*xl*	*xpl*	*xps*	*x s*	*xP*
exact	excellent	expel	expense	excess	export

xP	*xPs*	*x—*	*x—*	*x—*	*xç*
expert	express	extension	extent	extend	excuse

xpe	*xpa*	*xp—*	*xPs—*
experience	explain	explanation	expression

xc	*xc—*	*xcsv*	*xcam*
exclude	exclusion	exclusive	exclaim

Writing 'acc-' and 'ox-'

An initial A indicator may be added to indicate **'acc-'**, but this is not always necessary.

'xp	*'x*	*'xL'*	*'x s*	*'x S*
accept	accent	accelerate	access	accessory

120

Contemporary Shorthand

The prefix '**ox-**' may be similarly written, the indicator may often be omitted.

ꞏx	ꞏx′	ꞏx‿z	ꞏx‿z—	-xj
ox	oxide	oxidize	oxidization	oxygen

Practice A 15

1. ‿ *ws mps* ‿ *b Z* ⁻ᐟ *xc* 'm *h o.* ×
2. ‿ *w* x‿ᵔ ᐟ *ju* *blv* ᐟ ᐟᵔᵔᵔ ?
3. ꞏc *b* — *xc* *f hs* c—ꞏ ‿ ‿ *ʃa* ×
4. ꞏ ᐦᵔx *s* ꞏ *ms mR* *Jm* ‿ ꞏ *bc* ×
5. *jgg s* ᴜ *rG* ᔆ ꞏ *xL* *Fm* ⁻ *Xss* ᵥ

    1.   It was impossible to be sure of the exact amount he owes.
    2.   To what extent did the jury believe the evidence?
    3.   There can be no excuse for his actions in this affair.
    4.   An index is a most important element in a book.
    5.   Jogging is usually regarded as an excellent form of exercise.

Days and months

You will need to become familiar with writing the days and months and with expressing time. Mostly these are similar to the longhand abbreviations which you already use everyday so they should not present any difficulties. Notice how the word '*day*' can be expressed effectively by using the A vowel indicator (but often even this can be omitted). The proper noun indicator has been omitted in the following examples for clarity.

m‿ꞏ	‿ᵉꞏ	wᵉꞏ	‿s,	F,
Monday	Tuesday	Wednesday	Thursday	Friday
ꞏ‿ꞏ	ꞏ‿ꞏ	j‿	fb	Mj	'Pl ·
Saturday	Sunday	January	February	March	April

m,	j‿	j L	wgs	sp	ᴜ
May	June	July	August	September	October

121

Roy B. Tabor

November	December	today	yesterday

tomorrow	tonight	morning	afternoon	evening

Spring	Summer	Fall	Autumn	Winter

Practice A 16

1. ⌐ r 30⌐ ← 'Pl, ⌐ ' ⌐ ×
2. L m ⌐ ⌐ ⌐ ⌐ M ⌐ ×
3. ⌐ —x m⌐ l b h⌐ ⌐ E M⌐ ⌐
4. ⌐ ⌐ ws 'G' f ⌐ ls m⌐, ← m⌐ ⌐
5. ys⌐ ' ws S⌐ b ⌐ ' m — s Z ×

1. There are thirty days in April, June and November.
2. Let me take you to dinner tomorrow evening.
3. The next meeting will be held on Friday morning.
4. The deadline was agreed for the last Monday in May.
5. Yesterday I was certain but to-day I am not so sure.

Double vowels

Occasionally two vowels follow each other without forming a diphthong and so are sounded separately, eg., *create, radio, science* and *area*. Usually such words can be written following the general rules given, by writing the stressed vowel and omitting the unstressed (short) vowel.

diet	poem	science	period	riot

✓ *The double vowels 'ea' or 'io' are written as combination indicators; 'ea' E + A, and 'io' I + O.* In practice these are written as simple forms, a small 'v' the same size as other

Contemporary Shorthand

vowel indicators; use whichever is most convenient for the particular word outline.

*a*ᵥ	ᵥ	ᵥ	*fl*ᵥ	*pl*ᵥ	*u*ᵥ
area	idea	radio	folio	polio	urea

A final L sound may be indicated in the usual way, by writing the double vowel indicator through or below the line.

*a*ᵥ	*B*ᵥ	*se*ᵥ	*m*ᵥ	*Sm*ᵥ
aerial	burial	serial, cereal	material	ceremonial

The word ending '**-iate**' is indicated by writing the 'ia' combination vowel in the '-ate' position; other endings may be added.

'*Ps*ᵛ	ᵛ	*B*ᵛ	*csl*ᵛ	
appreciate	deviate	depreciate	conciliate	deviation
*C*ᵛ	*C*ᵛ	*r*ᵛ	*csl*ᵛ	
create	creation	radiation	conciliation	

Practice A 17

1. ╰ *s* — ⌐ ⌣ *mc* ' *f*ᵤ *cm* ⌣ *M*- ×
2. *z* ↗*w* ⌣ ╰ *ws* ' *f*ₘ *fw* ← *h*ᵦ *agm* ×
3. ↘ *z*⌐ — *v* ⌐ *eg* ⌢ ⌐*cg* ⌐*ug* ╲ *Lg* ×
4. ╰ *m*ᵍ ⌐ ← *cp*` *Gem* — *l* *s*ᵥ. ×
5. *z* ⌐ — ⌣ ⌣ ╰ *ws* ' *s*ᵨ *fcv* *sl*⌐ ×

1. There is no need to make an official comment until tomorrow.
2. She thought that there was a fundamental flaw in his argument.
3. They should not have been eating or drinking during the landing.

123

Roy B. Tabor

4. Their meeting ended in complete agreement on all issues.
5. She did not think that there was a single effective solution.

Initial vowels

A disjoined A-vowel may also indicate an initial **'ad-'** or **'ab-'**,

'js	*'js� *	*'jcv*	*'m*	*'v*	*'Vb*
adjust	adjacent	adjective	admit	adventure	adverb

✍ In words beginning with **'im-'** the initial vowel is usually omitted, but in words beginning with **'em-'** the initial vowel is always included.

m`	*mj—*	*mp,*	*mpm*	*mG—*
immediate	imagination	imply	implement	immigration

mf s	*m*	*Mj*	*Mj—*	*mG—*
emphasis	empty	emerge	emergency	emigration

See chapter 15 for other optional prefixes.

The '-us' ending

Short and unstressed vowels usually can be omitted in connected matter. It follows therefore, that a final S can indicate the word ending **'-us'**. (An S-circle may be used if preferred.)

cps	*—M s*	*fms*	*bo*	*j*
campus	numerous	famous	bonus	generous

Where a double vowel sound is formed with the **'-us'** ending as in **'-ious'**, it is indicated, as pronounced, by E + S; where necessary this may be disjoined. The S-circle is preferred.

cu	*se*	*fu*	*Pv*	*va*	*v*
curious	serious	furious	previous	various	devious

Contemporary Shorthand

In some words the vowel combination '**-ious**' is pronounced as 'shus', but which may be spelled variously as '-cious', '-tious' or '-xious' and occurring in such words as delicious, ambitious and anxious. In these words you write what you hear, SH ('z') + S (the S-circle is preferred).

⌐z₀	csz₀	⌐lz₀	Pz₀	Gaz₀
anxious	conscious	delicious	precious	gracious

Practice A 18

1. ` 'plc— ⁻ s↵ hs hlp⌐ ⌣ mPv O w₁ - lf ₓ
2. V⁻ ws cu₀ ⌣ L⌐ M bo h₀ ˈ⌐⌣. ₓ
3. ` gV̄m s˙ se₀ bo ⌣. mG— pls↘ ₓ
4. H ⌐⌣ ws ⌐z ⌣ c⌐₀ ` ⌐⌐m ₓ
5. ˈ v ⌣ 'm⌐ ⌣ ¹ ⌐sₘ pc⌐ s bg—g ⌣ ⌐Mj ₓ

1. The application of science has helped to improve our way of life.
2. Everyone was curious to learn more about his adventures.
3. The government is serious about its immigration policy.
4. Her doctor was anxious to continue the treatment.
5. You have to admit that a dismal picture is beginning to emerge.

The End of the Beginning

You have now completed your study of Alpha-level shorthand. If you have practised all the examples given and have been using the principles when making your own personal notes you should have increased your previous speed of writing longhand significantly. You will also have realized how simple and logical the system is and that you can customize it to suit your own way of writing.

But this is not the end of your potential for writing quick notes, it is only the end of the beginning. If you are writing notes

Roy B. Tabor

several times a week you will want to proceed to acquire some advanced techniques which will increase your writing speed even further.

With these advanced techniques you may again customize your note-taking by selecting those rules you wish to adopt. The opportunity is there for you to write at speeds in excess of 100 words a minute but you need to be aware that writing at such speeds is not merely a matter of learning the rules. The skill of high-speed writing is one of listening to the spoken word and carrying it in your memory while writing the previous sentence. This skill comes with a little practice but this shorthand method provides you with the necessary tools to achieve success.

How far you go is entirely in your own hands but this will be influenced by the frequency of your note-taking. The more often you write notes using shorthand the more familiar you will become with the system and the more skilled you will be in the use of this powerful system of fast writing.

Abbreviation principles

The general abbreviation principles of Basic mode are applicable at Alpha level (see chapter 16). These are optional at this level, but using them, together with the additional prefixes and suffixes, will increase your writing speed and will add more fun and achievement to your note-taking.

education	enthusiasm	certificate	impossible
approximately	equivalent	problem	individual
photograph	unanimous	particular	remarkable

Often only the root word need be written where the context provides the meaning.

confer, conference, conferring

urgent, urgency, urgently

Contemporary Shorthand

⌐F
differ, difference, different

sʃs
suggest, suggested, suggestion

s͜s
satisfy, satisfaction, satisfactory

oj͜
origin, original, originality

Prefixes and suffixes

All the prefixes and suffixes given in Part Two, Basic mode, chapters 18-19, also may be applied at Alpha level. Use your own familiar longhand letters as appropriate.

Numbers

All the notes and recommendations regarding the writing of numbers also apply at Alpha level. Where high writing speeds are not needed numbers may be written in your normal way. It is always important to record figures accurately and your familiar figures may be sometimes more appropriate. For more positive recognition numbers may be circled.

Roy B. Tabor

Part Four
Keyboard

Keyboard is a special version of this method of shorthand which is adapted to use only the characters found on a QWERTY keyboard. The basic word abbreviation rules, as used throughout the integr-ated system, apply; but only standard keyboard letters are typed.

Although writing notes with pen and paper is usually more practical, using a keyboard in certain circumstances may sometimes be preferred. It may be particularly attractive for lectures, whether at college, university or a conference venue, where some post-meeting work is expected to be done.

The keyboard can be very fast in creating letters or characters, but it has its own limitations. Hand-written Alpha-level uses longhand letters which can be blended with each other and used for specific abbreviation purposes. Such techniques are not available on the keyboard. Thus in some alphabetic systems either standard letter keys are given a second meaning or punctuation keys are given new and arbitrary meanings. In this shorthand method we avoid arbitrary signs and symbols. Consequently punctuation signs are used for their designated purpose and are not used to represent the sounds of speech. (The one exception is the use of the slash (/) to indicate the suffix '-*ly*'.)

Punctuation

✓ At the end of a sentence a double period point is used (..).

✓ Because capital letters have a particular meaning in Keyboard proper nouns are indicated by typing an 'equals' character

(=) at the end of the outline.
London *lndn*= New York *nu Yc*= Jane *jan*=

Contemporary Shorthand

Basic principles

The basic rules of Basic mode apply in writing Keyboard; any modifications to the rules will be mentioned as they apply.

☑ *Type each word as it sounds.*

☑ *Type the principal sounded consonants and omit short vowels in the body of a word.*

Indicating vowels

In Keyboard a normal vowel letter is typed in place of the special vowel indicators used in the hand-written levels. Initial and final vowels are included in the word outline. same *sam* team *tem* attack *atc* elephant *elfnt* unit *unt*

Note that a final 'ee' sound is indicated by the letter 'e', however the word is spelt. fee *fe* plea *ple* dummy *dme*

Quick forms

Group A comprises the most frequently occurring words.

a, an, and *a* ; be, by, but *b* ; can, come *c ;* do *d* ; the *e* ;
if, for *f* ; go, good *g* ; he, him *h* ; I *i* ; each *j* ; kind *k* ;
all, like, will *l* ; am, me, my *m* ; no, not, in *n* ; out, only *o*;
up, put *p* ; quick, quite *q* ; are *r*; is, so *s* ; to, it *t* ; you *u*;
have, very *v* ; we, with *w* ; except *x* ; why *y* ; she *z*.
Group B comprises other important words which occur very often.

after *af* ; again *ag* ; before *bf* ; came *ca* ; from *fm*;
off, often *of* ; only *on ;* today *td* ; that *tt* ; upon *pn ;*
which *wj ;* within *wn* ; yesterday *ys* ; would *wd* ; who *hu*.

Final T and D

In words where a final long vowel is followed by T or D, the consonant is omitted and the relevant vowel only is typed.

Roy B. Tabor

| wait | *wa* | meet | *me* | sight | *si* | note | *no* |
| made | *ma* | need | *ne* | side | *si* | rude | *ru* |

When T follows a final S the letter T is omitted.

| test | *ts* | best | *bs* | list | *ls* | latest | *las* |

Writing R

The general principle of the system to indicate R is to double the size of the preceding letter. In Keyboard the same principle is applied by typing a capital, or upper case, letter.

(You may prefer to type an 'R' rather than use the shift key.)
The sound of R is read after a capital or upper-case letter.

| dry | *Di* | try | *Ti* | drug | *Dg* | free | *Fe* |

Applying the rule that short and unstressed vowels are omitted,

| turn | *Tn* | more | *M* | court | *Ct* | sort | *St* |

When the intervening vowel is long a capital vowel is typed.

| care | *cA* | dare | *dA* | pure | *pU* |
| career | *CE* | cure | *cU* | lower | *lO* |

The following commonly occurring words use the R principle.

her *H* ; car *C* ; door *D* ; poor *P* ; your *U* ; other *T* ; sir *S* ; another *nT* ; ever, every *V ;* were *W* ; extra *X* ; certain *Stn*

H and the double consonants

Initial H is omitted in familiar words and where a long vowel follows.

home *om* hope *op* whole *ol*

Double consonants; TH, CH, SH, QU

The double consonants are represented by single letters.

TH is represented by the letter '*t*'

| this | *ts* | that | *tt* | these | *tes* | though | *to* |
| north | *Nt* | rhythm | *rtm* | method | *mtd* | rather | *rT* |

130

Contemporary Shorthand

CH is represented by the letter '*j*';

cheat *je*   chance *jns*   such *sj*   teacher *tJ*

SH is represented by the letter '*z*'.

she *z*   cash *cz*   shop *zp*   shrink *Znc*

Sure is indicated by an upper case '*Z*'.

sure *Z*   assure *aZ*   pressure *PZ*   censure *snZ*

Indicating diphthongs

The following diphthongs are given single distinctive letters.
'**I**' is represented by the letter '*i*'.
die *di* high *hi* try *Ti* tie *ti*
'**OW**' is represented by the letter '*o*'
out *o* ; town *ton* ; down *don* ; now *no* ; outside *osi* ; outcome *oc*
'**OI**' *is represented by the letter* '**y**'
boy *by* ; join *jyn* ; avoid *avy* ; choice *jys* ; point *py* ; appoint *apy*

Writing the sound of AW

The 'aw' sound in *raw, ball, haul* and *ought* is represented by
the letter '*w*'. A following T or D is omitted.

law *lw* ; saw *sw* ; raw *rw* ; caught *cw* ; taught *tw* ; fought *fw*

The prefix *auto-* can be easily indicated by *w-*, and *audio- by*
wd-. The hyphen indicates that the preceding letter is to be read as
a prefix.

automobile *w-mbl* ; automatic *w-mtc* ; audio-visual *wd-vsl*

Abbreviating principles

Many long words may be abbreviated by writing to the end of
the stressed syllable of the word.

particular	*Ptc*	certificate	*Stf*	unanimous	*unn*
equivalent	*eqv*	enthusiasm	*ntus*	necessary	*nss*
photograph	*foto*	approximately	*aPx*	adjustment	*ajs*

131

Roy B. Tabor

Root words

The root outline of a word may be used for its derivatives. Where necessary, or preferred, the final syllable may be added to these abbreviated words.

urgent, urgency, urgently	*Ujn*
satisfy, satisfaction, satisfactory	*sts*
origin, original, originality	*Ojn*
suggest, suggested, suggestion	*sjs*

Prefixes and Suffixes

The most frequently occurring prefixes and suffixes are simplified to a single significant letter.

con-, can-, com-: *c*
cancer   *cS*   concert   *cSt*   contact *ctc*   commit *cmt*

in-, en-, un-: *n*
enough   *nf*   enter   *nT*   invade   *nva*   inform   *nFm*
uncertain   *nStn*   unsure   *nZ*   unaware *nwA*

-ng: *g*
bring   *Bg*   being   *bg*   finger   *fG*   longer   *lG*
bringing   *Bgg*   belonging*blgg*   jungle   *jgl*   single   *sgl*

-ment, mount: *m*
document *dcum* moment   *mom*   departmental   *dPtml*

-tive: *v*
motive *mov*   active   *acv*   effective*efcv* relative *rlv*

The prefix '**re-**' is indicated by '*r*', and '**pre-**' by *P*.
return   *rTn* ; refer   *rF* ; pretend *Ptnd* ; pre-view*Pvu*

The ending '*-ly*', the common indicator of adverbs, is indicated by the slash sign /.
likely   *l/* ; quickly   *q/* ; slowly   *slo/*

Contemporary Shorthand

The 'shun' ending

The word ending pronounced as **'shun'** is indicated by the letter *'z'*

mention *mnz* action *acz* operation *oPz* condition *cdz*
nation *naz* suggestion *sjsz* practitioner *PctZ*
national *nzl* operational *oPzl* occasional *oczl*
The word ending pronounced as **'shunt'** is indicated by *'zt'*
sufficient *sfzt* efficient *efzt* efficiently *efzt'*

Writing X

The letter 'x' is also used for initial **'ex-'**
expense *xpns* export *xPt* exercise *Xsis* exert *Xt*

The Quick Form *except x* is used in associated words;
exception *xz* exceptional *xzl* exceptionally *xz/*

This initial 'x' may also be used to indicate **'acc-'** and **'ox-'**; the initial vowel may be included if necessary.
accept *xpt* access *xss* oxide *xi* oxygen *xjn*

Double vowels

There are a few words where two vowels follow each other without forming a diphthong, as in *create, radio* and *science.* Usually these words can be written by following the rules already given, that is, by writing the stressed vowel and omitting the unstressed vowel.

science *sins* riot *rit* prior *PI* period *Ped*
diet *di* poem *pom* theory *tEe* area *Aea*

More prefixes and suffixes

A hyphen indicator, '-', may be used to indicate specifically that a prefix or suffix is intended.

Roy B. Tabor

Prefixes

extra-: *x-*
extra time *x-tim* extra value *x-vlu* extra work *x-Wc*

over-: *o-*
overall *o-l* overtake *o-tac* oversight *o-si*
under-: *u-*
understand *u-stnd* understood *u-std* undergo *u-g*

electr-: *el-*
electric *el-c* electronic *el-nc* electricity *el-se*

trans-: *T-*
transfer *T-F* transmit *T-mt* transaction *T-acz*

circum-: *Sc-*
circumference *Sc-Fns* circumstantial *Sc-stnz*
but note circumstance *Sc* circumstances *Scs*

super-: *su-*
supermarket *su-Mct* superintend *su-ntnd* superficial *su-fzl*

Suffixes

-self: *-f*
himself *h-f* herself *H-f* itself *t-f*
myself *m-f* yourself *U-f* ourselves *O-fs*

-graph: *-g*
photograph *fo-g* telegraph *tl-g* monograph *mn-g*

photography *fo-ge* geography *je-ge* calligraphy *cl-ge*
geographical *je-gc* biographical *bi-gc*

-ology: *-j*
biology *bi-j* apology *ap-j* geology *je-j*
psychologist *sic-js* zoologist *zu-js* dermatologist *Dmt-js*
biological *bi-jl* pathological *pt-jl* psychological *sic-jl*

-ification: *-fc*
specification *sps-fc* modification *md-fc* notification *no-fc*
classification *cls-fc* qualification *ql-fc* justification *js-fc*

-bility: -be

ability	*a-be*	possibility	*ps-be*	capability	*cp-be*
reliability	*rli-be*	visibility	*vs-be*	adaptability	*adp-be*

-lity: -l

legality	*lg-l*	formality	*Fm-l*	personality	*Psn-l*
senility	*sn-l*	facility	*fs-l*	agility	*aj-l*

Writing numbers

Ordinals may be indicated by typing a hyphen after the figure.

first / 1st *1-* second / 2nd *2-* third / 3rd *3-* fourth / 4th *4-*

The adverbial form is indicated by using the '-ly' suffix indicator /
firstly *1/* secondly *2/* thirdly *3/* fourthly *4/*

Preparations for note-taking

Always be well prepared for a keyboard note-taking session. The following points are worth noting.

- Create at least two new files on your hard drive to which your notes can be saved.
- Give these files names which are descriptive of the meeting; avoid such names as 'Meeting 1' or 'temp'.
- Always include the date, either in the file name or at the head of the notes. The former practice is safer as you may forget in the flurry at start of the meeting.

Roy B. Tabor

Writing Keyboard manually

Users of Keyboard who wish to write notes with pen and paper may do so with a few modifications. This uses only the minimum, essential rules of the integrated system.

- All consonants are written in their normal longhand form.
- Vowel indicators are used instead of their longhand forms except when the R sound follows.
- When R follows a long vowel, lower case vowel letters are written; *care **ca** near **ne** fire **fi** pure **pu***
- The suffix '-ly' is indicated by writing the E-indicator below the line.
- The = sign for a proper noun is written below the word outline.
- The hyphen indicator for prefixes and suffixes is omitted.

These modifications follow the rules of Alpha-level. However, writing standard Alpha-level is usually preferred where the use of the simplified letters, D, T and N, greatly increases the speed of writing.

Contemporary Shorthand

Part Five
Reading and writing practice

These additional practice pieces may be used after completing the relevant chapters in the textbook, OR you may use them for revision purposes when you have completed the full course.

Read the following phrases and sentences as quickly as you can.

Then turn to the relevant key and write the phrases and sentences in your shorthand notebook. Your first attempt should aim for accurate and neat outlines. Check your outlines against those given here.

Repeat this procedure writing more quickly each time. The more often you repeat this the more fluent you will become in reading and writing. Fast reading is more important than fast writing, so go back over these practice pieces until you can read all of them as quickly as you can read normal print.

Read / Write Practice 1. Writing T and D. (Complete chapter 6 first)

1.
2.
3.
4.
5.
6.
7.
8.
9.
10.

Roy B. Tabor

Read / Write Practice 2. The sounds of R and S. (complete chapter 8 first.)

1.

2.

3.

4.

5.

6.

7.

8.

9.

10.

Read / Write Practice 3. Writing L. (complete chapter 9 first.)

1.

2.

3.

4.

5.

6.

7.

8.

9.

10.

Contemporary Shorthand

Read / Write Practice 4. Writing H, CH and SH.
(complete chapter 10 first.)

1.
2.
3.
4.
5.
6.
7.
8.
9.
10.

Read / Write Practice 5. Diphthongs. (complete chapter 12 first.)

1.
2.
3.
4.
5.
6.
7.
8.
9.
10.

Roy B. Tabor

Read / Write Practice 6. The TR principle. (complete chapter 17 first.)

1.
2.
3.
4.
5.
6.
7.
8.
9.
10.

Read / Write Practice 7. (complete chapter 19 first.)

1.
2.
3.
4.
5.
6.
7.
8.
9.
10.

Contemporary Shorthand

Read / Write Practice 8. Laughter and Mountains.

Laughter.

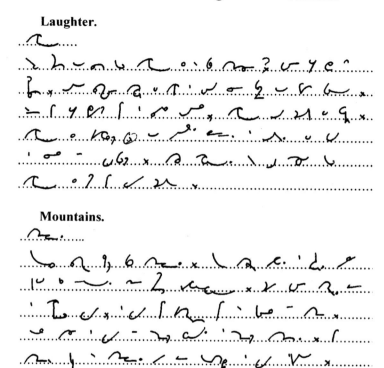

Mountains.

Roy B. Tabor

Read / Write Practice 9.

Bright eyes.

(shorthand text)

Nursing.

(shorthand text)

Journeys.

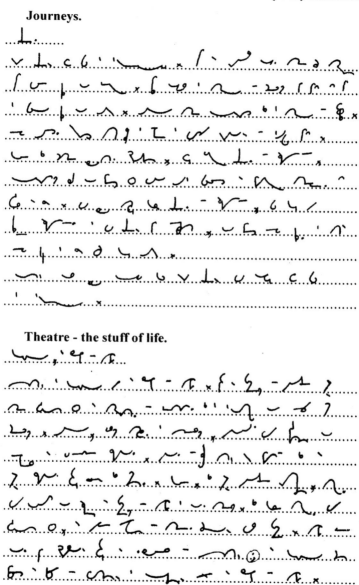

Theatre - the stuff of life.

Roy B. Tabor

Keys to Read / Write Practices.

Read / Write Practice 1. Writing T and D.
1. I would like to know what can I do for you.
2. This is the time for you to let go.
3. Is that true, can I quote you on that?
4. You do know that I have quit the habit.
5. 6. What have you got to do today?
6. Did you mean to let the cat out of the bag?
7. What time do you want to go to visit your son?
8. I will wait for you tonight at the bend in the road.
9. Did you want to go for a ride with him?
10. The rent is due today, have you paid it yet?

Read / Write Practice 2. The sounds of R and S.
1. I have sent my daughter a birthday card.
2. It is a a matter of grave concern to us.
3. I am sorry, but you will have to grin and bear it.
4. I am sure that she will give them a perfect answer.
5. I think that he only pretends to be kind.
6. What is the surname which appears on his passport?
7. I suggest you take a closer look at what she has done.
8. I am quite sure that you deserve better than this.
9. In any case I would like to pursue the matter further.
10. We are certain of what the result will be this time.

Read / Write Practice 3. Writing L.
1. What a time to fall in love!
2. Can you find the musical clue to the puzzle?
3. I cannot believe that of my own flesh and blood.
4. The world has become a global village.
5. I have a wonderful feeling about this.
6. Please will you clean up this mess without delay.
7. I think you are in real trouble over this affair.
8. We need to check her dental records for forensic purposes.
9. She has given birth to identical twins at the hospital.
10. Right now I will settle for a simple glass of water.

Contemporary Shorthand

Read / Write Practice 4. Writing H, CH and SH.
1. I am afraid that this is too hot to handle.
2. Do you think that he can kick the habit this time?
3. The twins played a clever game of chess.
4. The police said that he had been shot in the chest.
5. You will need to shake the bottle well before use.
6. That was such a foolish thing you did.
7. There is a basic right of no taxation without representation.
8. My son has an addiction to all kinds of science-fiction.
9. Did I mention that I have a serious heart condition?
10. We have received an invitation to her wedding reception.

Read / Write Practice 5. Diphthongs.
1. I am sure that was the wrong thing to do.
2. We all agree that there is something to sing about.
3. I do not know how you can tolerate that clown.
4. Do you want to make an announcement?
5. He will be with us in just a moment.
6. The postponement of the event has been a great disappointment.
7. Several important amendments have been made to the document.
8. Only a portion of the consignment has been received.
9. We believe that a monumental error has been made in this matter.
10. It is said to be a fundamental element of their belief.

145

Read / Write Practice 6. The TR principle.

1. There is always an alternative interpretation in such cases.
2. That is a very controversial suggestion which is difficult to accept.
3. He is a picture of intense concentration.
4. What is the central theme of the film?
5. That was such a wasteful extravagance.
6. She introduced him to the exciting world of literature.
7. Both the exterior and interior of the car are very clean.
8. The injured animal showed extreme signs of distress.
9. What an extraordinary idea, can it be true?
10. It would seem that he has contravened the regulations.

Read / Write Practice 7.

1. There is a time to speak and a time for silence.
2. Nothing can equal the beauty of truth.
3. We have been told that he who hesitates is lost.
4. Friends don't let their friends drink and drive.
5. Birds of a feather flock together.
6. It's a long road that has no turning.
7. A good wife is worth her weight in gold.
8. Good little girls go to Heaven, the others go to Las Vegas.
9. Marriage is like a lottery, the tickets are cheap but you never win.
10. Most men can be trusted - and all pigs can fly.

Laughter.

Have you heard it said that laughter is the best medicine? When you are sick or depressed let some-one make you laugh and you will soon begin to feel better. Even if you are suffering from a serious illness, laughter will help you cope. Laughter is relaxing; it releases tensions and leaves you with a sense of well-being. Most doctors have little doubt that laughter is good for your health.

Mountains.

There is something special about mountains. Their massive rocks and peaks rise upwards as nature's own grand architecture.

Within the mountains one moves in a different world, a world far removed from the pettiness of men. It is also a world of changing colours and changing moods. For many people the mountains are in themselves, a world apart.

Bright eyes.

It has been said that the eyes are the mirror of the soul. If you want to know how a person is thinking, look into the eyes; the eyes will reflect the truth. Your eyes are also a measure of your health; bright eyes indicate good health, but dull eyes suggest poor health. Any lover will tell you that the eyes are worth looking into.

Nursing.

Nursing is all about caring and if one thing is certain, it is that nurses care. They care enough to train hard in order to become skilled in nursing methods and techniques. A good nurse gets to know her patient and tries to bring comfort and normality when one is sick or in pain. Nursing is a truly caring profession and nurses play an important part in society.

Journeys.

Every journey can be an adventure. From the earliest times man has moved from one place to another. First it was a matter of hunting for food or for a better place to live. Later man traveled as a matter of conquest, new lands provided more space and often a wider variety of available food. Then, as human settlements developed, came other journeys of exploration, traveling just to find out what lay beyond the further mountains or across the sea. We still make these journeys of exploration, but they are personal explorations and we journey for enjoyment, to find new places and meet new people and see how they live. Today it is still true that every journey we take can be an adventure.

Theatre, the stuff of life.

Drama and theatre are the stuff of life. Before the beginning of religion early man acted out the movements of animals as an attempt to ensure good hunting. Later, using masks and dancing, rituals were performed to influence the unknown spirits. Rites of passage may have followed as the early spirits became seen as

Roy B. Tabor

gods. Then, as early religion emerged, myths were told to explain the beginning of life and its meaning. As those myths were acted out the record of man's history was begun, Life in its full diversity became the substance of drama; the theatre had found the power of comedy and tragedy – the stuff of life.

About the Author

The author has spent many years developing this contemporary approach to writing shorthand. A retired medical librarian, he has experienced the needs of people taking notes at meetings, and of students in undergraduate and postgraduate education.

After extensive research into older and existing shorthand systems he has evaluated techniques and methods. His conclusions are presented in this work; a unique integrated method of shorthand which can be written at two levels, one for the professional shorthand writer and another 'alphabetic' level for the general note-taker.

Printed in the United Kingdom
by Lightning Source UK Ltd.
111048UKS00001B/36